HEALING AND WHOLENESS

HEALING AND WHOLENESS

by
John A. Sanford

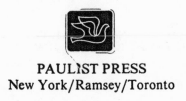

PAULIST PRESS
New York/Ramsey/Toronto

Unless otherwise indicated, all biblical references are from the Jerusalem Bible, copyright © 1966 by Darton Longman & Todd, Ltd. and Doubleday & Company, Inc.

Library of Congress
Catalog Card Number: 77-83576

ISBN: 0-8091-2044-5 (paper)
ISBN: 0-8091-0225-0 (cloth)

Published by Paulist Press
Editorial Office: 1865 Broadway, New York, N.Y. 10023
Business Office: 545 Island Road, Ramsey, N.J. 07446

Printed and bound in the
United States of America

Contents

ACKNOWLEDGMENTS

I wish to thank the many people who helped make this book possible. First, my gratitude to my wife, Linny, to whom this book is dedicated, who listened for many hours as I read this manuscript, and made many helpful suggestions. My thanks also to Helen Macey, whose editorial assistance was invaluable, and to the Reverend Morton T. Kelsey who made some vitally important suggestions. My appreciation also to Robert P. Sedgwick, M.D., and Stuart Dadmun, M.D., who read the manuscript, particularly with an eye for medical details, and made many important suggestions. Last but not least, my gratitude goes to the many people who have consulted me over the years with regard to finding healing, and who generously allowed me to mention a bit of their stories in this book.

To My Wife, Linny

Introduction

We hear a lot about healing today. Methods of healing are proclaimed from many different directions. The health care field grows and grows. More money is spent on health each year; more persons enter the health care field. Medical science develops by leaps and bounds, but more esoteric methods of healing also enter the field. We hear of holistic medicine, body therapies, the healing value of various types of meditation. There is an abundance of therapies of all sorts, some making modest claims to be helpful, others messianic in their promises. Methods of healing through clay, art, dance, sand play, yoga, and a host of others are urged upon us.

There is a plethora of psychiatrists, psychologists, pastoral counselors, marriage counselors, psychic healers, spiritual healers, and various types of lay healers springing up among us. Even the churches have reentered the field of healing, not the mainline of Christendom, to be sure, but sizable numbers of Christians are involved in a grassroots movement that seeks to explore healing through prayer and the religious life.

Yet at the same time our overall health does not seem to improve. The increase in longevity, won by victories over childhood diseases and the achievements of the new science of immunology, has slowed to a halt. In America, particularly, life expectancy no longer increases significantly, and we rank well down on the list of nations in terms of longevity in spite of our medical care system. Today we simply die from different causes than we did yesterday. Smallpox, the great scourge of mankind in past centuries, is now on the verge of extinction, the last known cases being in isolated villages in Ethiopia. Puerperal fever, tuberculosis, typhoid fever, polio, and numerous other infectious diseases have receded into the background as the great killers. In World War II not a single American soldier died of tetanus;[1] only eighty years earlier, in the Civil War, tetanus was as much feared as the bullets of the enemy. Today heart disease, cancer, diseases of the circulatory system (which include arteriosclerotic vascular diseases), accidents, cirrhosis of the liver, and suicide head the list of killers.[2] Strangely enough, among primitive people such as the American Indians, death from these causes was exceedingly rare. In

1

spite of our advancing knowledge the key to increased health and well-being has not been found; only the symptoms of the problem are changing.

Of course our way of life, our so-called civilization, is clearly taking its toll. Our mechanization, the anxiety and stress under which we live, our alienation from our neighbors and ourselves, the pollution of our environment, the built-in hazards of our modern diet, and, perhaps most of all, the haunting sense of meaninglessness that stalks many of us today are taking their toll of our physical and psychological well-being. Perhaps the reason for the almost fantastic explosion of interest in healing that we witness today stems from our need to find a way to live a healthy life in a physical and psychological environment full of new dangers.

We can find almost any approach to healing that we desire. Some approaches, for instance, avoid religion like the plague; healing is to be found through science, or through a purely humanistic approach. Other approaches declare that only God brings healing and are suspicious of any healing method in which God, at least as He is conceived, is not the central focus. In psychology, at one end of the spectrum, we have the behaviorists, with their rigidly narrow scientific standards; on the other extreme we have C. G. Jung, who does not hesitate to proclaim that man is a spiritual being. Jung is in an especially strange position today. He is rejected by the Establishment of psychiatry and psychology as a "mystic" because he sees the religious nature of the soul, but he is equally rejected by religious groups because of what is seen to be his "unorthodoxy." Yet it is to Jung that more and more lay people are turning, and, often in secret, some professionals too, because Jung offers the hope of finding meaning again.

The stream of human knowledge is like a great river; many streams and rivulets make up its volume. Of course not every prophet of healing today contributes to our knowledge, for some are fraudulent, their waters polluted, and some dry up and never reach the flowing river of valid human knowledge. Yet it remains true that we must expect insights from many different sources if our knowledge of the source of healing is to grow. Hopefully this book will add one more rivulet to our stream of knowledge. It is itself a composite of many sources, enriched by the sufferings and discoveries of the people who have consulted me over the years, the insights into healing given to me by many mentors, and the fruit of my own personal search for healing. It also draws upon insights into healing from wells ancient and modern: ancient Greek healing mysteries, the lore of shamanism, the wisdom of the American Indian, the healing emphasis in early Christianity, and the very modern perspective on healing furnished by C. G. Jung. The hope is that the reader will, through this book, see a little more clearly where healing comes from, and where he or she as a person can learn to help himself or herself. But it is not a complete book on healing nor does it pretend to be. There is far more to be said about healing than this book, or any one book, can say, though hopefully the reader will find some insights that are new and helpful.

Before we can meaningfully discuss healing, however, we need to know what constitutes illness and what constitutes health. What does it mean to be ill? What does it mean to be healthy? This is where we must begin.

Notes

1. Ronald J. Glasser, M.D., *The Body Is The Hero* (New York: Random House, 1976), p. 127.

2. From the 1975 records of the Vital Statistics Division of the San Diego County Health Department.

I
Journey toward Wholeness

Illness is something that results in a malfunctioning of consciousness.[1] The center of consciousness is the *ego*, the "I" part of us that does the willing, suffering, choosing in life; the part of us of which we are most immediately aware. If this part of us is not able to function, it would seem that we are ill. So this definition of illness seems to fit. It is neat, to the point, and seems accurate. Any of us who has had even the flu can identify with this definition. We lie in bed enervated, wracked with fever; we are dizzy when we stand up, and we lack energy. Clearly our ego, under these conditions, is malfunctioning and we are experiencing what it means to be sick.

Psychological distress can be equally incapacitating. Depression or anxiety can cripple us; we can become overwhelmed by psychic contents and virtually unable to function. Such psychological states can be every bit as painful as physical maladies and they, too, can be called forms of illness since they result in our "malfunctioning." It seems clear, then, that painfulness and incapacitation are a part of illness and a way to identify it.

However, the matter is not quite as simple as it might seem. The malfunctioning of consciousness of which I have spoken is characterized by its painful quality, but sometimes the pain is not felt by the person who is ill, but by others. That puts illness in a different light.

There are people who are characterized by arrogance, brutality, or a pathological lack of conscience. They are unaware of their true condition, or if they are aware of it they may not care. To all intents and purposes such a person does not suffer, but others who come into that person's path do. Under certain conditions, such as a position of power, the arrogant, brutal person seems to get along splendidly. He carries out life's requirements with admirable efficiency, and he would certainly reject the idea that he is ill. Only others, upon whom he inflicts his inner disorder, would speak about such a person's illness.

Convicted mass killer Richard Speck is an obvious example. When asked about his crime, in which he executed eight nurses,

Speck is reported to have said that he didn't do it. The *Los Angeles Times* reports that Speck "still insists that 'I ain't never killed nobody,' " which is what he steadfastly maintained at his trial, despite the fact that one Filipino nurse lived to identify him and that his fingerprints were all over the room.[2] Obviously the illness in this man is not something he experiences as his personal pain and failure, but is to be seen in those on whom his illness is inflicted.

A more subtle example of the way in which the effects of one person's illness may be observed in others is the case of the "family casualty." As the late noted psychotherapist Frances Wickes has shown, it sometimes happens that psychological problems and conflicts in a family may appear in one of the children when they are not faced consciously by the parents.[3] In such a case the hidden illness of the family becomes visible in the child. There is a force within us that always works to bring things into the light. If parents are not conscious of their own darkness, the burden of their own psyches, the unrecognized problems may appear in one of the children who serves as a scapegoat and carries the psychological ills of the family.

Not all the difficulties children experience can be laid at the door of the parents' repression of their own problems. Each person carries into life his or her own particular fate, and there are many circumstances that contribute to the shaping of the psychology of each individual. Nevertheless, such family casualty cases do exist, and they illustrate that while illness results in pain, the true source and cause of the pain may not always be apparent.

It would seem, then, that this matter of illness is not as clear as it appeared at first. We may not always be able to measure our own state of health, for it may be precisely the person who refuses to recognize his illness who is the greatest carrier of it. In psychological matters especially there are many Typhoid Marys.

Perhaps we can understand more completely what constitutes illness if we understand what health means. Here our language helps us. The word "health" is derived from the old Saxon word "hal," from which we get the words "hale" and "whole." When we say "hello" to someone we mean we hope they are *hal* or whole. So health seems to be wholeness.

Wholeness implies something organic, that is, many separate parts working together in a unified way. The body is a good example of organic wholeness. Our kidneys, heart, lungs, liver, pancreas, nervous system, and the other parts of the body are all designed to function together, and make up a wonderful unity. To say the wholeness of the body is organic means that if any one part of the body suffers the whole body suffers. If something is wrong with a kidney, for instance, we feel ill all over; we do not just feel ill in the kidney. Without the healthy functioning of the kidney, the entire body suffers and, in fact, will eventually die.

The same thing is true of the psyche or personality. The personality is every bit as varied and complex as the body. If a portion of our true nature is denied, we suffer throughout. We cannot afford to exclude anything that belongs to us, thinking that in this way we have rid ourselves of a problem, for whatever we have denied suffers, and this suffering of the part affects the whole.

This truth is expressed by Jesus in the parable of the Lost Sheep in which he says, "Tell me. Suppose a man has a hundred sheep and one of them strays; will he not leave the ninety-nine on the hillside and go in search of the stray? I tell you solemnly, if he finds it, it gives him more joy than do the ninety-nine that did not stray at all." (Mt. 18:12-14) This parable, and its companion, the parable of the Lost Coin (Luke 15:8-9), emphasizes the importance of *the whole*. Without the full one hundred sheep the wholeness, which the number one hundred represents, is missing. Spiritually, the ninety-nine themselves are not complete without the missing one. This is the nature of totality.

Of course the personality and the body are not separate realities, but together make up the complete human being. For this reason a physical disorder affects our personality, and what goes on in the personality also affects the health of the body, as psychosomatic medicine demonstrates. So the *whole* human being is a remarkable unity of the body, with its various parts and functions, and the psyche or personality, with its equally diverse aspects. The healthy person would thus seem to be the one in whom all these myriad parts are functioning harmoniously.

Of course this is scarcely a new thought. Ancient Greek medicine, for instance, regarded all illness, physical or psychological, as the result of a loss of harmony. It was believed that as long as man was in harmony with himself and the gods his life was whole and in balance, and that illness was the symptom of a loss of balance and harmony. American Indian healing rests upon much the same idea. The Navajo sand painter, for instance, reconstructs the harmony of the universe in his sand painting, and seeks to restore his patient to health by making him a part of the essential harmony and wholeness of all life which the sand painting expresses.

Well and good, but how do we know when we are whole? "Peace of mind" suggests itself as a mark of wholeness. It is certainly something many people seek. Some years ago a book with this title sold millions of copies, and today forms of meditation and numerous religious systems attempt to sell themselves to us with their promises to bring us "peace of mind." Obviously we would not have to look so hard for something if it were not something we lacked. Perhaps if we were whole we would have this peace of mind, and not have to suffer so much.

Yet, curiously enough, if there is one thing the great men and women of history have *not* been noted for, it is peace of mind. All the way from Jesus of Nazareth sweating drops of blood in the Garden of Gethsemane to Abraham Lincoln sunk in his brooding depression at the time of the Civil War, peace of mind has not been something we remember as a quality in great people. Greatness seems to be born out of pain, conflict, and struggle, not out of peace, unless it is the final "peace which passes all understanding," that ecstatic sense of oneness that comes as a gift of God to the struggling soul. St. Gregory of Nyssa once declared, "The soul who is troubled is near unto God." It sounds as though it is not peace of mind that brings us to wholeness, but struggle and conflict, and spiritual enlightenment occurs only when a person has been through dark and disturbing trials of the soul.

This also suggests that while illness results in pain, pain is not necessarily a symptom of illness. Our present culture is an anti-pain culture. We do anything we can to escape life's pain, and the resources of drugs and alcohol are always nearby to help us to do so. This overlooks the importance of carrying pain correctly as part of the process of becoming a whole person. The emergence of the whole person is also the crucifixion of the individual ego, and often the pain that we experience is as much the birthpain of wholeness as it is a symptom of illness.

If peace of mind is not the hallmark of wholeness, perhaps adjustment is. Like peace of mind, "being adjusted" is something highly prized in our society. From the conventional, clinical point of view, to be healthy is to be adjusted, and the goal of most therapy is to return a person to a satisfactory mode of functioning in society. "Satisfactory" adjustment is equated with a state of functioning in which a person does not draw attention to himself. "Unsatisfactory" adjustment usually means that a person's behavior or attitudes have become conspicuous to others in a dangerous, annoying, or disturbing way.

Unsatisfactory ways of adjusting may include *maladjustment* and *nonadjustment*. Maladjustment covers those people who constitute a danger to others. Examples would be criminal activity, murderous behavior, sociopathic personalities. Nonadjustment would refer to those people who are no more dangerous to others than anyone else, but who cannot cope with life, or who annoy or disturb others by their behavior and attitudes.

In our society we categorize the first type, the maladjusted, as criminals or, at the least, as people with "character disorders." The second class of people we label as "ill," and we may confine them to various institutions, supposedly for treatment but, at least in some cases, simply to get them out of sight.

An example of the latter type of case is the story of Kenneth Donaldson, a 67 year old Florida man who was confined for fifteen years involuntarily in state or county mental institutions. Donaldson suffered from delusions and hallucinations and was confined for these many years at the original instigation of his father. He was not so crazy, however, that he did not struggle through many court hearings in an effort to win his freedom, finally carrying his case to the Supreme Court. Donaldson argued that he was not dangerous to others, that he was receiving only custodial care and not treatment, and that he was being illegally denied his personal, physical freedom. In a ruling of the Supreme Court in 1975, it was declared that a person who was mentally ill but harmless to others could not be confined against his will so long as he could survive in freedom, unless it could be shown that effective psychotherapeutic treatment would be made available. Curiously enough, Donaldson had more difficulty winning his freedom than many criminally inclined people who win early paroles and promptly repeat their crimes against others. One can't help but wonder if, in our society, there is a secret identification with the violence of the criminal, and a corresponding fear among us of the emergence of the unconscious in the hallucinations and delusions, however harmless they may be, of men such as Donaldson.

Donaldson was identified as mentally ill because he had curious psychological experiences others did not have. He saw things others did not see, and so drew unfavorable attention to himself. It bothers us when such people are around. We declare that they are not adjusted, though in fact the problem may be that they threaten *our* adjustment. But this *adjustment* of which we speak is exceedingly important to most of us in deciding who is healthy and who is not, so important that the goal of many forms of therapy is to enable a person to become a "well-adjusted" member of society.

In types of therapy having such a goal, if the suffering person can once again function in society without drawing attention to himself in too drastic a manner, that person is considered cured. In some cases drugs may be used this way. Drugs may be effective in helping a person adjust because they are often able to alleviate anxiety, relieve depression, and submerge disturbing emotions. Psychopharmacology has a battery of drugs of various kinds that can be used to enable a person to adjust without troublesome emotion to a variety of situations. In the hands of a competent and careful doctor, drugs can be helpful in enabling patients, who would otherwise hopelessly deteriorate or regress, to lead a semblance of a natural life. Or, they may be used creatively as an adjunct to psychotherapy to stave off a threatened psychosis or suicide until the psychotherapy can become effective. But all too often the philosophy behind the use of drugs is to give them indiscriminately to alleviate painful psychological states; when given in such a way they produce a kind of adjustment, but impede psychological progress. The fact that drugs are used in this way so widely indicates how many therapists there are who are oriented to the philosophy of adjustment, and how many patients there are who want to be treated in this way.

Electric shock therapy is also an example of an adjustment-oriented therapy. When administered in large doses, shock therapy is said by many to result in permanent loss of memory and impairment of the capacity for emotional reaction. Patients often complain that part of their personality has been destroyed by electric shock. However, shock therapy frequently does relieve, at least temporarily, incapacitating depressive states, and suppresses patterns of behavior that are troublesome to society. For these reasons, electric shock therapists regard this treatment as beneficial, and its negative side effects are either ignored or depreciated. If "adjustment" is the goal, the use of shock therapy may be justifiable.

Behavioral modification is another example of a form of therapy that rests upon the model of adjustment. Behavioral modification attacks a person's disturbing symptom directly, in the belief that if the presenting symptom or disturbance can be changed, the individual will be adjusted, and hence well. Behavioral modification therapy may be at its best when it is aimed at a specific problem. One psychiatrist friend of mine, for instance, reported that he referred a patient for behavioral modification who was literally eating herself to death. Already grossly overweight, this patient was adding about five pounds per week and it seemed as though nothing could stop her. If behavioral modification is able to alleviate this specific, distressing problem, it will have been useful, but generally behavior modification becomes a kind of philosophy in itself. Then *health* and *adjustment* are so equated that the ultimate goal seems to be for society to decree what is to be regarded as acceptable behavior and, through behavior modification, condition everyone to adjust to that standard. The result would be "perfect health," since health is defined in terms of perfect adjustment.

The idea of adjustment also plays a central role in various religious denominations. Most of our established religions encourage people to accept a particular religious doctrine, ritual, and way of life, and reward that individual by including him as an accepted member of a particular religious community. Such a total acceptance of a religious system is regarded as "faith," and the person who is able to accept all that is offered to him with little or no doubt, struggle, or dissent, is a faithful member. Such religious systems exist, of course, because there are so many people who want them to exist. Just as many people go for certain kinds of therapy hoping to be readjusted to life with a minimum of pain, so people create, and turn to, religious systems hoping to find one to which they can adjust and so find that peace of mind and sense of security of which we spoke earlier. Any religious system that can offer us total adjustment to life with a diminution of pain and struggle will win an immediate following.

The positive values of adjustment cannot be overlooked. The individual who is mal- or nonadjusted is often a problem to himself and to others. The nonadjusted person may welcome *any* form of therapy that enables him to function again in life. It is no fun to feel crippled by depression or anxiety, and readjustment to a certain level of functioning is often a goal that is desired by patient, therapist, and society alike. It is also, sometimes, all we can hope to accomplish in certain cases. As long as society and human nature are what they are, there will always be a place for such forms of treatment.

However, in our society it is easy to go too far in the direction of adjustment, especially when it comes to institutional care for the emotionally disturbed. In a rare departure from heavily drug-oriented treatment programs for the mentally ill, John W. Perry, M.D. and Howard Levene, M.D. of San Francisco have experimented with a drug-free program for acutely psychotic young adults, age 18 to 35. The fundamental philosophy of this program, which Dr. Perry calls Diabasis, from a Greek word meaning "crossing over" or "passage," is the belief that the human psyche has a self-healing tendency, a thesis which we will explore more fully as this book develops, and that an acute psychosis is in fact an attempt on the part of the psyche to bring about a healthy reorganization of the personality.[4] With this idea in mind, Drs. Perry and Levene created a residential facility, staffed by trained paraprofessionals, which provided a safe and understanding environment, in which the acute psychosis of the six or eight residents was allowed to run its course. No drugs, shock treatment, or other forms of external therapy were used. Out of thirteen clients who remained in the program over two weeks, ten made an "excellent" recovery, followed by effective living and self-support, and only two required later hospitalization. Unfortunately, Diabasis was funded by the government and the funding was terminated after only eleven months of operation. A "Diabasis II" is now under way, this time with private funds to ensure that it is not prematurely terminated.

Dr. Perry was encouraged in this unique attempt to provide a healing environment for the mentally disturbed by a research project at Agnews State Hospital in San Jose, California, from 1969-1971. Designed by Drs. Julian Silverman and Maurice Rappaport, the project was carried out on a specially created experimental ward of the hospital. The subjects of the experiment were one hundred and twenty-seven young males who had suffered acute schizophrenic episodes. One hundred and eight of these were studied for a period of three years after being discharged from the project. The subjects were assigned at random to either of two groups: a chlorpromazine treatment group (an anti-psychotic medication), or a placebo group (unmedicated pills). The experiment was "double blind," meaning that neither staff members nor patients knew which persons were receiving the drugs and which the placebos. The medicated patients showed faster reduction of psychotic symptomatology than did the unmedicated patients, as was to be expected. However, during the follow-up period the unmedicated persons were found to suffer less severity of illness, while medicated patients, whether they continued to use drugs or not, were found to have greater functional impairment. Furthermore, it was found that, overall, significantly fewer patients who had been given placebos had to return to the hospital than those who were medicated. To be exact, the rate of recidivism among those who were medicated was 83%, but only 8% among those who were given placebos and were not placed on medication during the follow-up period.

These experiments suggest that in some cases, in opting for adjustment versus health we may in fact be perpetuating illness. Of course, it should be noted that the subjects of the experiments were acutely psychotic and that these findings do not apply to the degenerative or paranoid psychoses. Nevertheless, these findings point out that when we talk of the values of adjustment we must ask the question "adjustment to what?" The assumption is that the adjustment is to life as we find it in our society. But what if the society itself is sick? What if a whole way of life is meaningless and cut off from spiritual roots? If an individual adjusts to a sick situation, the individual can only become a part of that sickness, even though from the point of view of the society in question he is "well."

The society of Nazi Germany prior to and during World War II comes to mind. That there was a terrible sickness in Germany at that time is clear from the dreadful atrocities of the concentration camps, and the virulent aggression that led to the death of some thirty million people during that war. People who adapted to Hitler's Germany of the 1930's appeared "well"; in terms of their particular social framework they were well adapted people. Those who could *not* adapt found themselves in a painful condition, and suffered a terrible malaise. They appeared to be the sick and disturbed people, but their very lack of adaptation may well have been a sign of their health. It is as though there was too much health in them to adapt to a sick situation.

An example is given by a Jungian analyst who found herself caught in Berlin during World War II.[5] She reports the case of a Nazi fighter pilot, a man 22 years of age, who was referred to her for analytical treatment because he had developed hysterical color blindness; although there was nothing organically wrong with him, he could no longer distinguish colors, and consequently was unable to fly. Because of his hysterical color blindness he could see everything only in black and white. She writes of him: "Analysis was rough going at first. The patient was cooperative but entirely uncomprehending. His philosophy of life had no room for dynamics hidden behind simple facts. Everything that was useful to Germany, Hitler and the victory, was good; everything else was bad. It was as simple as that—black and white."

This young man had been raised in Hitler's Germany and had made a complete identification with the Third Reich and the Hitler Youth Movement. Until his color blindness developed, he was a completely adapted person, functioning superbly; he was "well." Only after his color blindness developed was he ill-adapted and therefore so "sick" he had to be sent to the doctor. He had a brother and a sister in his family. His brother he adored; he was a member of the SS and an ideal Nazi. His sister he hated, for she had joined the underground resistance and, in his eyes, was a despised traitor.

Eventually the young pilot had dreams. He found them puzzling and disturbing, for in his dreams everything seemed to be reversed from the way it should have been. He dreamt, for instance, of his beloved brother: "He was wearing his SS dress uniform," he related, "but everything was the wrong way. The uniform was white instead of black, and his face was entirely black. It was just the opposite of life." Then he dreamt of his sister; in his dream his sister was dressed in black prison garb, but her face was shining white. The young pilot commented, "I could have understood if the face had been black for that would have shown her guilt."

After being confronted with the fact that in his dreams his brother's face was black, and his sister's shining white, he observed, "So the dreams do change everything around. They make the good appear black and the bad white." Then, the analyst noted, he made a further and very important comment about the uniforms. It did not matter to him whether a prison garb was good or a uniform bad for "the outside appearance does not matter; it's the face that's important." The analyst observed, "The patient did not then know that he had already started to differentiate between outside and inside—between the persona, expressing the outside reality, and the face, the expression of the inside reality."

Some time after these dreams he was with his adored brother, who was then stationed at a concentration camp. The brother had drunk too much and in his drunkenness talked about what was going on at the concentration camp. That night the young man dreamt, "A long column of concentration camp inmates with radiant white faces marched past Hitler. Hitler's face was black and he raised his hand, the color of which was the deep red color of blood." The patient put this dream in a letter and mailed it to his analyst with the note that he was going to visit the concentration camp and find out for himself what was going on. His confidence in his beliefs was finally shaken under the impact of the dreams, and an individual desire to know for himself was beginning to work. "I have to find out for myself," he said in his note.

Not long afterwards, the analyst related, another note came from the young pilot. It said simply, "I believed too long that black was white. Now the many colors of the world won't help me any more." The analyst never saw him again. He had committed suicide.

No doubt the German military intended that the analyst would "cure" this young pilot so he could return to useful military service. But the patient's unconscious had other plans—to bring about consciousness. The analyst bravely aided the creative forces of the patient's own unconscious, no doubt at considerable personal risk.

Eventually consciousness *did* break through. When the symptom of the color blindness lay hold on the young pilot, he was beginning to experience a movement from within toward health. What looked from the outside like illness and symptomatology was, viewed from the inside, a move to consciousness and wholeness. He could only become healthy by *losing* his adaptation and falling "ill." At the moment when he became conscious, he achieved true health; at his moment of greatest nonadaptation he achieved his greatest spiritual and psychological wholeness. But the consequences of his newfound consciousness were intolerable. The annihilation of the old ego with its false beliefs, and the seeming impossibility of any longer existing in his Nazi Germany, were too much for him and he committed suicide. We usually think of suicide as a sign of profound illness; yet in this case the suicide came because of health, but health was something the young man could not endure.

It would seem, then, that illness *is* a malfunctioning of consciousness, and health *is* wholeness, which means an organic unity and balance of all the forces within a person. But the *measure* of malfunctioning and the *measure* of wholeness is not something either the individual ego or society has in its possession. Some individuals who seemingly function well, and would refute the idea that they were ill, are, judged from the viewpoint of others, ill people whose disorder brings great pain upon their fellows. A society may also be ill. Although I used Nazi Germany as an example of a sick society, there is plenty of evidence that our entire Western culture has much illness in it.

"Peace of mind" as a standard for wholeness may amount to nothing more than anesthetization of the individual's higher sensibilities to himself and his surroundings. Truly great people have never had much peace of mind, for they were too aware of their own inner conflicts, of the pain and suffering around them, and of their own calling to a life of struggle. Adaptation as a standard of wholeness is also misleading if it is the society in which a person lives that measures the adaptation. If the individual adapts to a sick situation, he becomes a part of that sickness. His *health* may then consist in a movement from within that actually results in what appears to be maladaptation to his surroundings and way of life. What constitutes our wholeness is not known to us consciously, and what a given individual, or society, declares to be the mark of health may actually be a monstrous error.

The case of our Nazi aviator, however, suggests that what constitutes wholeness is known to the unconscious mind. The dreams of this patient turned everything upside down. From the time that his color blindness developed, it is clear that something within this young man that he did not know about was seeking to establish in him a new awareness. His wholeness was known, not to him, nor to his Nazi superiors, but to the unconscious.

Deep inside each organism is something that knows what that organism's true nature and life goal is. It is as though there is within each person an inner Center that knows what constitutes health. If our conscious personality becomes related to this inner Center, the whole person may begin to emerge, even though this may not bring either peace or social adaptation, but conflict and stress. The collision between the conscious personality, and its desire to conform with a minimum of pain to the collective demands and expectations of society, and the demands from the inner Center for wholeness may result in painful symptomatology as a necessary, inevitable prelude to a development toward health. The movement toward health may look more like a crucifixion than adaptation or peace of mind.

The Swiss psychologist C. G. Jung called this movement toward wholeness "individuation," and felt it was the source of all true health. Individuation is the process that moves one to become a completed, unique person. As we will see in a later chapter, this means the synthesis of the conscious and the unconscious personalities, and the establishment of a relationship between the ego, as the center of consciousness, and what Jung called the *Self*, which is the whole personality and which functions like our inmost Center. Individuation is a living process that leads *toward* wholeness but, at least in this lifetime, is never completed, for the whole personality is never actually reached. Wholeness calls for the fulfillment of our potentiality, but this can never be achieved, for human potentiality is too rich, and the demands of life upon us are constantly changing and calling forth new responses. The whole person is an ideal that can never be realized. Nevertheless, what it means for us to be whole seems to be known in the unconscious Center of our being, and it is from this Center that the process of individuation is begun. We do not "decide" to become whole; rather it is thrust upon us by the life force within us.

To speak of individuation is to give a scientific name to a process that is at work in all of life. Every living organism seeks its proper goal, and this is individuation. The acorn has its inner pattern and if it develops into a mighty oak tree we could say that it has individuated. Acorns always become oak trees and never pine trees because each living thing can become only what it is meant to be. We either become what we are meant to be or are a caricature of our true self,

the process

an incomplete, distorted version of what was to be our true reality. Everything in nature seeks to realize itself, and that is what individuation is all about.

The tiger in the jungle is naturally whole. He has no difficulty being a tiger; he simply is what he is meant to be. He has no guilt when he kills the deer for that is what tigers are meant to do. Only with man is it different, for in man the life process that seeks its realization must develop through a conscious personality. Unless our conscious personality develops and increases, and becomes a channel for the life of the whole person to flow through, the process of individuation cannot take place. And if this happens, and the life's energies that seek to bring about wholeness are dammed and thwarted, they may turn against us. A creative life not realized becomes poisoned. Nature, when thwarted, takes her own revenge. In this, as we shall see in the next chapter, lies the potential for illness.

blockage generates illness / disease

The individuation process did not wait for psychology to come along before it happened; it has always been seeking to happen in life, and has been recognized by perceptive spirits of all time. The great religions of the world are deeply concerned with individuation, each speaking in its own way, using its own cultural forms. Here, for instance, is the way the Sioux Indian holy man Lame Deer speaks:

"Medicine men—the herb healers as well as our holy men—all have their own personal ways of acting according to their visions. The Great Spirit wants people to be different. He makes a person love a particular animal, tree or herb. He makes people feel drawn to a certain favorite spot on this earth where they experience a special sense of well-being, saying to themselves, 'That's a spot which makes me happy, where I belong.' The Great Spirit is one, yet he is many. He is part of the sun and the sun is a part of him. He can be in a thunderbird or in an animal or plant.

"A human being too is many things. Whatever makes up the air, the earth, the herbs, the stones is also part of our bodies. We must learn to be different, to feel and taste the manifold things that are us. The animals and plants are taught by Wakan Tanka (the Great Spirit) what to do. They are not all alike. Birds are different from each other. Some build nests and some don't. Some animals live in holes, others in caves, others in bushes. Some get along without any kind of home.

"Even animals of the same kind—two deer, two owls—will behave differently from each other. Even your daughter's little pet hamsters, they all have their own ways. I have studied many plants. The leaves of one plant, on the same stem—none is exactly alike. On all the earth there is not one leaf that is exactly like another. The Great Spirit likes it that way. He only sketches out the path of life roughly for all the creatures on earth, shows them where to go, where to arrive at, but leaves them to find their own way to get there. He wants them to act independently according to their nature, to the urges in each of them.

"If Wakan Tanka likes the plants, the animals, even little mice and bugs to do this, how much more will he abhor people being alike, doing the same thing, getting up at the same time, putting on the same kind of store-bought clothes, riding the same subway, working in the same office at the same job with their eyes on the same clock, and, worst of all, thinking alike all the time. All creatures exist for a purpose. Even an ant knows what that purpose is—not with its brain, but somehow it knows. Only human beings have come to a point where they no longer know why they exist. They don't use their brains, and they have forgotten the secret knowledge of their bodies, their senses, or their dreams. They don't use the knowledge the spirit has put into every one of them; they are not even aware of this, and so they stumble along blindly on the road to nowhere—a paved highway which they themselves bulldoze and make smooth so that they can get faster to the big, empty hole which they'll find at the end, waiting to swallow them up."[6]

"A human being is many things. . . . We must learn to be different, to feel and taste the manifold things that are us. . . . The leaves on one plant—none is exactly like another. . . . All creatures exist for a purpose. . . . Only human beings . . . don't use the knowledge the spirit has put into every one of them." These words describe individuation. They talk about the process of becoming whole which depth psychology perceives and tries to elucidate. It is a process of fulfilling the unique life which is in every one of us, a paradoxical experience in which we come to know our common humanity on the one hand (where we are like everyone else), and our uniqueness on the other hand (where there is no one else quite like us). It is a process, as Lame Deer says, that every ant knows, but which human beings can know only if they consult "the secret knowledge of their bodies, their senses, and their dreams."

In one sense, each person who walks the path of wholeness walks a familiar path trod by all those men and women from untold thousands of years who have become what they were meant to be. So we find the trail is there for us, and there are signs and guides on the way, but at the same time each of us is one of life's experiments. Our particular personality, our particular way, our particular set of life circumstances have never been tried before. Life experiments with us in its ceaseless attempt to bring about new and more unique forms. In this way evolution continues.

As we have seen, the whole person we are meant to become is unknown to us consciously. Nevertheless, our potential wholeness, the goal of our development, lives within us as a dynamic potentiality that profoundly influences the course of our lives. Only gradually, in the course of a lifetime of development, living, and contemplation, can we become aware of what it means to be ourselves. But to say that something exists in the unconscious is not to deny its reality and power. On the contrary, the most powerful forces in life emanate from the unconscious, a lesson mankind has yet to learn, for through the unconscious flow those energies that shape life for better or worse, and always there is the attempt of our unseen Center to bring about the complete man or woman.

It is impossible to summarize the way a person becomes whole. It is, for one thing, an individual matter, differing with each person. But it can be said that to become whole we must be involved with life. This earthly existence appears to be a crucible in which the forging of the whole person is to take place. Our life must have a story to it if we are to become whole, and this means we must come up against something; otherwise a story can't take place. Some people seem destined to become whole by combating outer life circumstances, some through encountering the inner forces of the unconscious, some through involvement with both. But if we stand on the sidelines of life, wholeness cannot emerge. If we are to become whole, we will have led a life in which darkness has been faced, and an encounter with evil has been risked.

This seems to be the paradoxical truth at the heart of the story in the seventh chapter of Luke's Gospel. Jesus is dining in the home of a Pharisee when a woman comes in who has an evil reputation, and, weeping in gratitude, washes Jesus' feet with her tears and dries them with her hair. The Pharisee, knowing of her bad reputation, criticizes Jesus to himself, but Jesus, intuiting what he is thinking, rebukes him. "Simon," Jesus says to him, "you see this woman? I came into your house, and you poured no water over my feet, but she has poured out her tears over my feet and wiped them away with her hair. You gave me no kiss, but she has been covering my feet with kisses ever since I came in. You did not anoint my head with oil, but she has anointed my feet with ointment." Then Jesus continues with a paradoxical statement, "For this reason I tell you that her sins, her many sins, must have been forgiven her, or she would not have shown such great love. It is the man who is forgiven little who shows little love." (Luke 7:36-50)

Jung seems to be stating much the same truth when he writes, "When one follows the path of individuation, when one lives one's own life, one must take mistakes into the bargain; life would not be complete without them. There is no guarantee—not for a single moment—that we will not fall into error or stumble into deadly peril. We may think there is a sure road. But that would be the road of death. Then nothing happens any longer—at any rate, not the right things. Anyone who takes the sure road is as good as dead."[7]

People who undergo the individuation process find themselves constantly thrown into doubt. If we wish certainties in life, we should not seek to become whole. Those who are convinced they possess the whole truth are precisely those who will miss it, for only those who know they lack the truth will seek it. Sometimes we are no longer sure where God is in our lives. We feel like Kazantzakis when he wrote, "Someone came. Surely it was God, God . . . or was it the devil? Who can tell them apart? They exchange faces, God sometimes becomes all darkness, the devil all light, and the mind of man is left in a muddle."[8]

Good and evil will be curiously intermingled in any meaningful life process. If we are to become whole, life will send us, not what we want, but what we need in order to grow. The forces of evil will have to touch our lives for without the dark Luciferian power, consciousness does not emerge, as Mephistopheles seems to be saying in Goethe's play *Faust* when he declares of himself that he is "part of that Force which would do evil ever, yet forever works the good."[9]

Individuation is a work, a life opus, a task that calls upon us not to avoid life's difficulties and dangers, but to perceive the meaning in the pattern of events that form our lives. Life's supreme achievement may be to see the thread that connects together the events, dreams, and relationships that have made up the fabric of our existence. Individuation is a search for and discovery of meaning, not a meaning we consciously devise, but the meaning embedded in life itself. It will confront us with many demands, for the unconscious, as Jung once wrote, "always tries to produce an impossible situation in order to force the individual to bring out his very best."[10]

Becoming whole does not mean being perfect, but being completed. It does not necessarily mean happiness, but growth. It is often painful, but, fortunately, it is never boring. It is not getting out of life what we think we want, but is the development and purification of the soul.

To be healthy, then, has nothing to do with serenity, and less to do with adjustment; to be healthy means to become whole. We can, perhaps, say that the truly healthy person is the person who is involved in the lifelong process of individuation. This gives us a point of departure for studying the meaning of illness, and understanding the process of healing. Perhaps when we look at illness and health from the perspective of individuation we can find the correct attitude toward them, and come to see more clearly what it means to be ill, what it means to be well, and, perhaps, even what it means to die.

Notes

1. For an amplification of this thought, see the article "Remembering C. G. Jung" by James Kirsch, M.D., of Los Angeles, in *Psychological Perspectives*, Spring, 1975.

2. See the editorial section of the *Los Angeles Times* for June 2, 1976.

3. Frances Wickes, *The Inner World of Childhood* (New York: Appleton-Century, 1927, revised and republished by Signet, 1968), chapter II.

4. Cf. the books by John Weir Perry, M.D., *The Self in Psychotic Process*, University of California Press, 1953; *Lord of the Four Quarters: Myths of the Royal Fathers*, Braziller, 1965; *The Far Side of Madness*, Prentice-Hall, 1974; *Roots of Renewal In Myth and Madness: The Meaning of Psychotic Episodes*, Jossey-Bass Publishers, 1976.

Data on the program at Agnews State Hospital is found in an article "Schizophrenics for Whom Phenothiazines are Contraindicated or Unnecessary." (1976). For further information write to Maurice Rappaport, M.D., Research Department, Agnews State Hospital, San Jose, California 95114.

5. Anneliese Aumuller, *Spring* Magazine, 1950.

6. John Lame Deer and Richard Erdoes, *Lame Deer, Seeker of Visions* (New York: Simon and Schuster, 1972), pp. 156-157.

7. C. G. Jung, *Memories, Dreams, Reflections* (New York: Random House, 1961), p. 297.

8. Nikos Kazantzakis, *The Last Temptations of Christ* (New York: Simon and Schuster, 1960), p. 15.

9. Goethe, *Faust,* trans. Charles E. Passage (Indianapolis, Ind.: Bobb, Merrill Co., 1965), p. 49.

10. C. G. Jung, "The Interpretation of Visions," *SPRING* 1962, p. 154.

II

Body, Soul, and Wholeness

Each culture has its own attitude toward illness and health. In the Old Testament, for instance, it was believed that if you were ill and suffering it was because of sin. God, being good and just, would not allow a righteous man to suffer. To be healthy and wealthy was thus a mark of favor from God, and, conversely, poverty and illness were the just deserts of sin. This is why Job's three "friends" who come to comfort him in his afflication wind up preaching to him. They can't stand the fact that Job refuses to accept the blame for his misfortunes, and maintains his righteousness. One of them, Zophar, says:

> "Is babbling to go without an answer?
>   Is wordiness in man a proof of right?
> Do you think your talking strikes men dumb,
>   will you jeer with no one to refute you?
> These were your words, 'My way of life is faultless,
>   and in your eyes I am free from blame.'
> But if God had a mind to speak,
>   to open his lips and give you answer,
> were he to show you the secrets of wisdom
>   which put all cleverness to shame—
> you would know it is *for sin* he calls you to account."
>
> (Job 11:1-6; italics mine)

This attitude lingered for a long time in the sin culture of the Biblical world. We find it again, for instance, in the ninth chapter of John's Gospel in the story of the healing of a man who was blind from birth. As Jesus and his disciples pass by the man born blind the disciples ask, "Rabbi, who sinned, this man or his parents, for him to have been born blind?" (John 9:1). Jesus' answer shows that he rejected this conventional attitude toward illness: "Neither he nor his parents sinned, he was born blind so that the works of God might be displayed in him."[1] (John 9:3)

22

In other ancient cultures, as we saw in the first chapter, illness was regarded as a loss of harmony. The soul in harmony with itself and nature would be whole, and illness was a sign that harmony of a man with himself and his cosmos was disrupted. This led to an emphasis upon health rather than upon disease. In other words, the whole person was the focus of the healing activity of the doctor or shaman for it was believed that if one became whole again he would be cured of his malady. This is in contrast to our culture in which the medical doctor is oriented to disease, not toward health, and the emphasis is upon treating specific maladies rather than upon working toward a whole, healthy person.

In the East the idea of karma influences the attitude toward illness. If a person is ill it is his karma. His accumulated karma from past lives has led to the need for this particular fate in this life. It is not quite as personalistic a condemnation of illness as we find in the Old Testament; there is no image of a God personally visiting illness upon the unrighteous. Rather, it is a spiritual law that karma must be fulfilled, and if one's karma demands illness and disease, that is the way it is. Taken to extremes this leads to a lack of interest in alleviating one's neighbor of his sufferings, for to do so might be to interfere with karma.

Our own culture has varying attitudes toward illness, most of them ill-founded prejudices. In some quarters the Old Testament attitude that illness is a result of sin reappears in a subtle way. For instance, among people who are involved in the spiritual healing movement (healing through prayer and faith) sometimes there is an insinuation that if a person is sick it is because that person lacks the requisite faith; if only that person had faith, or were more spiritually developed, the sickness would not exist. A variant of this occurs in people who espouse the idea that what happens to you is always a result of your own thoughts. Taken to extremes, this attitude can lead people to look down upon those who are ill and harbor the secret thought, "They would not be ill if only they had the right thoughts." For the more fortunate, such attitudes linking sickness with sin or wrong-thinking lead all too easily to a feeling of spiritual superiority, while for the person who is ill they add guilt to the sufferings already brought on by the illness.

In other quarters it is believed that if one is physically ill, it is all right, but if one is psychologically ill it is not. Here the view is that we are not responsible for our physical illnesses; these are matters of fate and do not reflect upon us personally. But if a person should show signs of psychological or emotional distress, something is wrong with that person himself. He is somehow responsible for such a condition, as though it is the result of some weakness of character or personality.

This may be why many psychotherapists find that referrals from doctors often are not successful. A conscientious medical doctor may perceive that his patient's illness or symptoms are connected to psychological and emotional problems and so refer to the counselor, but the counselor usually discovers that such people seldom stay in therapy to work through any problems. They have gone to the medical doctor in the first place because they wanted to believe that their problems were physical and could be cured by medical means. To go to the psychotherapist is to admit that something is wrong with *them*, and it is precisely this realization that they wish to avoid. In this case it is shame that operates, rather than guilt. The reasoning seems to be that one need not be ashamed if one is physically ill, but one does feel ashamed if one is psychologically distressed.

Recently in our culture there is a growing movement to reevaluate our attitudes toward illness and health. Heroic efforts are being made to show that mental distress is an illness on the same footing as any other; that there is no reason to be ashamed if one suffers from anxiety, depression, or other psychological maladies. There is also a growing emphasis upon what makes for health, a helpful counterbalance against the overemphasis upon disease that has already been mentioned. Researches into a healthy, nutritional diet, the beneficial effects of physical exercise, and the healthful influence of spiritual exercises of many sorts are being studied as part of a resurgence of interest in the development of healthy men and women. This seems to connect to the ancient view that if a person is in harmony with himself and his world he will be healthy.

Out of all this there is emerging the realization that we are to be our own doctors as far as maintaining health is concerned. The medical doctor is needed when symptoms of disease have started, but responsibility for maintaining our health belongs to us. This is a good counterbalance to a past tendency to elevate the doctor to the position of an authority in matters of health, and a present recognition that whether or not we are and will remain healthy may partly depend upon *our* attitudes, way of life, and spiritual and physical resources.

In spite of these positive trends, there is still no adequate theory in our time of the meaning of illness and health. However the realization that the purpose of life is to produce wholeness gives us a new perspective from which to view the meaning of illness, health, and even death. We know very little about these matters, but it is possible to raise questions and suggest ideas that may, in the future, bear fruit.

One exceedingly fruitful area for study lies in psychosomatic medicine. In some ways, psychosomatic medicine is extremely ancient. Primitive peoples, for instance, believed that physical illnesses were caused by spiritual problems, loss of soul, or invasion by a demonic agency. We have already noted that the Greeks stressed the connection between the psyche and the soma. Jesus declared,

> "The lamp of the body is the eye. It follows that if your eye is sound, your whole body will be filled with light. But if your eye is diseased, your whole body will be all darkness. If then, the light inside you is darkness, what darkness that will be!" (Matt. 6:22-23)

The "eye" in this saying is clearly symbolic of spiritual or psychological perception. The "body" might be a symbol for the whole self, not simply the physical body; nevertheless, the saying does suggest that if our psychological perception is diseased, that is, if we do not see ourselves and reality clearly, it fills the whole self, and the body too, with darkness. Perhaps spiritual evil and physical disease result from this.

Although the connection of psyche and soma with regard to health is something mankind has long known existed, all too little has been done in recent times in this field. To be sure, certain diseases and physical symptoms, such as ulcers, colitis, high blood pressure (under certain conditions), headaches, and lower back pains are usually regarded by doctors as psychosomatic in origin, and some physicians go so far as to believe that virtually all physical disorders have a psychogenic basis. These are rare, however, and it is even rarer that the general public sees a connection between a physical disorder and the state of one's soul. Most physicians simply treat the physical symptoms and let the psychic state of their patients take care of itself. That is not neglect on their part. As we have seen, medical doctors are mainly trained to treat disease, not to promote health. We do not have a culture like that of the ancient Chinese in which the doctor was paid when everyone in the community was well, and was chastised when people became ill, and whose healing herbs were not intended to cure symptoms as such but to correct imbalances between the body's yin and yang forces.[2] To a certain extent our health is up to us, and we cannot expect too much of the medical doctor, who is generally consulted only when things have gone too far anyhow.

could people to learn to care for themselves?

Yet, curiously enough, the main killers of today (listed in the Introduction) may be mostly, or all, psychological and spiritual in origin. We may have replaced the infectious diseases, which were the great killers of yesterday, and which modern medical science has dealt with so brilliantly, with killers that are born out of the soul. Heart disease, for instance, seems to be greatly influenced by lack of exercise, improper diet, and smoking, yet people continue to lead unhealthy lives almost as though there was a secret wish in them for death rather than for life. Cancer is also felt by many researchers to be psychological in origin, one theory being that it occurs when psychological life fails to develop properly, especially when a person has met with the loss of a person whom he or she loved, or has some other object (such as a job) taken away so that libido has been drastically drawn out of life. Cancer seems to have been exceedingly rare among people like the American Indians, so much so that it is called the disease of civilization, suggesting that there are pronounced psychological, spiritual, and environmental factors that are its cause. As with heart disease, so with many forms of cancer, smoking is a major factor. Yet people who know of the acute danger to their health continue to smoke, which points to complex and powerful psychological factors. Accidents have long been known to be connected to psychological problems. Flanders Dunbar, for instance, estimated that eighty percent of the major accidents that occur each year are directly related to the personality of the victim.[3] Cirrhosis of the liver comes mainly from alcoholism, a spiritual problem par excellence, and, of course, suicide is manifestly a psychological and spiritual problem.

So although too little is known about the connection between spirit and body, there are many facts suggesting that there is a profound connection between the two. In what follows I wish to mention a few cases and thoughts that bear upon the hypothesis that health is a matter of psyche and soma. These are, of course, merely illustrations of possibilities. I am aware that the "anecdotal" approach I will be using *proves* nothing, but it does suggest lines along which further research may be indicated.

C. G. Jung often suggested the connection between somatic illness and the problems going on in the psyche, and was especially interested in the possibility that dreams might announce, diagnose, or even prescribe for physical illnesses. He felt, for instance, that cancer was associated with an unsolved problem of psychological development,[4] and his writings contain many helpful allusions to the connection between dreams and illness. In one of his letters, Jung comments on the case of a young man who had been stricken with poliomyelitis at the age of four and who recalled an impressive dream that occurred just before his illness. "He dreamt he was sitting at his mother's feet," Jung writes, "playing with some toy or other. Suddenly a wasp flew out of the mother, which stung him, and immediately he felt his whole body poisoned and he awoke in terror." He adds, "I knew the patient's mother and she was a very domineering personality and a burden to her children."[5] We seldom have records of dreams that precede major illnesses, but Jung's example suggests there may be a definite connection.

Some examples from my own work and experience may help. A young man who was deeply involved in his process of development was determined to get a Ph.D. in his chosen field. He worked for a year to accumulate the necessary undergraduate requirements and made application to the proper graduate schools. It was, however, in his particular case, a goal that came from his ego, a desire to gain power and prestige, and his unconscious was against it. He began to develop distressing symptoms: nervousness, irritability, chronic anxiety, hunger, and painful twitches in the facial area. Eventually these symptoms drove him to his doctor. The painful facial symptoms were laid to a harpes virus, an infection of the sheathing around the nerves which can be exceedingly painful. The symptoms of irritability and nervousness were ascribed to a hyperactive thyroid. His doctor decided to treat the thyroid condition with radioactive iodine reserving more radical forms of treatment for a last resort.

The young man related, "As soon as the doctor told me I had a hyperactive thyroid I knew that this was because I was insisting on pursuing my goal of getting a Ph.D." At this same time the young man had frightening dreams. In one dream, for instance, there was a great cobra that loomed menacingly above him. He recognized these as warning dreams, and now he knew his physical symptoms were also warning him that he was going counter to the intent of the unconscious. "That very day the doctor told me what was wrong with me," the young man stated, "I decided to give up my goal of graduate work." Within two weeks of this decision all of his symptoms vanished. His thyroid returned to normal and has been normal ever since. It is known that hyperthyroidism often follows emotional trauma, and that remissions occasionally occur. This story hints at some of the psychological tensions that might underly such a disease, and the kinds of shift in attitude that might favor a remission.

There is little doubt in the mind of this man that his somatic disorders were the result of a conscious decision to pursue a goal that was not part of his individuation and that had been rejected by the

unconscious. Had he persisted in his goal he now believes he would
have developed a permanently diseased thyroid. Fortunately for him
his respect for the power of the unconscious was great enough that,
once persuaded his plans were against his own nature, he changed his
course in life.

Whenever we go against nature we pay a price, for we are ourselves a part of nature. Individuation, this matter of becoming whole,
is a part of our natural process. If we are called to wholeness, and
then persist in a path that is counter to the intentions of our deepest
Self, we pay a price. Of course we know this physically. If we persist
in smoking we may well develop lung cancer; if we jump off a cliff we
can expect to break a leg; we cannot abuse the body without paying
for it physically. The same is true of the psyche. If we go against our
own psychic nature a price has to be paid, and for some people the
price may be somatic illness. Generally this happens when the individuation process is not consciously experienced but has been rejected and driven into the body in a negative and disturbing way.

A man of about forty years of age had suffered from an ulcer for
many years. Eventually the ulcer began to bleed and the doctors
operated, removing part of his stomach and performing a vagotomy
(severance of the nerve that connects the brain and the stomach). This
made it virtually impossible for his ulcer to return, and after a long
convalescence he began to improve markedly. For a brief time I was
close to this man, and was able to see him gradually improve. After
the operation he had looked like a walking skeleton, but slowly his
body renewed itself, he put on healthy weight again, and began once
more to show that he could have a strong body. Then, in a way that
was unaccountable to me, he lost his spiritual perspective. He began
to drink and several years after his operation had become an alcoholic, and died in a few years. His psychological problems were deep; he
was a very wounded person. He never could get at the deep psychic
wound in himself, and the ulcer seemed to be an expression of it.
When, as a result of his surgery, he no longer had an ulcer, his
psychic illness apparently had to appear again in another form.

Another man who suffered from an ulcer also had radical surgery virtually preventing the ulcer from returning. But within a few
years he was dead of cancer of the liver. There is always the possibility that this man had a cancerous ulcer, and that the cancer metas-
tasized and eventually reappeared in the liver. No such report, however, was made to the family, and the more likely possibility seems to
be that whatever psychological and spiritual problem had become
somatized in the ulcer eventually developed into the cancer. This, at

least, must be taken as a distinct possibility.

A woman in her thirties had had sixteen surgeries in her brief life, many of them major ones. Her physical condition was complicated, and she had once suffered from tuberculosis. Eventually she could no longer find any physician who would operate on her. She had a veritable compulsion to be operated upon, and when this was no longer possible, she took her own life. She, too, was a deeply injured person. Somehow successive surgeries had become for her a life necessity. Perhaps what she really needed was surgery on her soul, a radical psychological operation, but would not, or could not, bring herself to do this.

A beautiful young woman died tragically in an automobile accident. It was a one-car crash and she had been driving, which always arouses the suspicion that conscious or unconscious suicide motives may have been involved. Her body was horribly mangled and the catastrophe could hardly have been more unsettling. Her father wept over the death of his daughter. He insisted on seeing her torn body saying that until he did so it would not be real to him. His grief was deep, but he bore the pain of it. Her mother didn't shed a tear. "It was God's will to take her back to heaven," she kept saying. She adopted the attitude that one should trust God's wisdom and keep a stiff upper lip. Two years after the death of the young woman her mother was buried; she had died of cancer. As I stood at the graveside with her husband he said to me, "You know, if my wife had only wept when our daughter died she would not be dead now."

The above case gives credence to the hypothesis mentioned before, that at least certain types of cancer may be induced by the loss of a person or object in which our life's energies have been involved. This unfortunate woman found no substitute for her lost daughter, and perhaps felt deeply rejected as well. There is certainly reason to believe that her husband was correct that her death resulted from her inability to overcome the problems that overtook her when her daughter died, and that the cancer was produced because of her failure to face up to reality, especially the reality of her own emotions. She had not faced the grief and rejection she felt at the death of her daughter, and perhaps this was the reason the cells of her body went wild and destroyed her. Her husband was a laborer, and not at all sophisticated, but he instinctively seemed to know that the death of his wife came because of her inability to face the painful events of their daughter's death.

A young woman in her early twenties came to see me because of a virulent case of acne. Her entire face was covered with one of the worst cases of acne I have ever seen. Her doctor had told her that, while he could treat her symptoms, the cause of the skin outbreak was psychogenic and she should seek help. This is what brought her to me. The skin condition was so distressing that during our first hour together she did practically nothing but weep. But in the next two or three sessions things began to emerge, and, like a miracle, within about three weeks from the time of her first visit her skin was entirely clear. One would never have known the acne existed. During our talks many things came to light. It was as though the unconscious was struggling to come up into consciousness, and things she had refused to face were demanding recognition. The psyche, denied recognition by consciousness, forced its way into the open by producing a skin eruption. There was no way she could avoid seeing the raw sores on her face that the acne produced. The psyche chose this way to force her to do something about herself, and come to terms with painful matters she had tried to avoid.

Anyone in the field of healing could cite examples such as these. It is possible that in all of these cases an illness was produced because a process that called for psychological development was denied. In those cases where a cure resulted, the somatic situation changed for the better once the psyche's demands for admission into consciousness were accepted. The suggestion is that sometimes somatic illness may result when a process of individuation has been blocked.

This may also be true of alcoholism. In a letter to "William," one of the two co-founders of Alcoholics Anonymous, C. G. Jung wrote that alcoholism was the result of a hungering for wholeness on a low level.[6] This means that underneath the craving for alcohol is the urge to individuation, but it is all so unconscious that the urge to wholeness takes the form of compulsive drinking. That being the case one can see why the alcoholic refuses to give up his drinking: it has as much grip on him as the individuation process itself; he is as bound to alcohol as he is bound to the cross of his own self-development. For the alcoholic to give up the demon of alcohol that has possessed him, he must find the greater spirit manifested in the urge to wholeness. As Jung put it in his letter, only one spirit can drive out another. The program of Alcoholics Anonymous is so successful with many alcoholics precisely because it does offer a spiritual orientation, and puts its members on the path to individuation.

In many cases of physical illness it seems as if the psyche was forced into the body causing the distressing symptoms. In two of the examples just given, in which there was a cure, the course of the somatic illness had not, fortunately, gone too far, and the psychological problems were not far from consciousness. Unfortunately, in most cases of physical illness the psychological problems have been driven deeply into the body, and the conscious resistance toward the psyche is so great that it is difficult to make these problems conscious. It is regarded as a physical problem, as though the psyche did not exist. If we could learn to listen to our bodies, and realize they are giving us information we need to know via the symptoms, the situation might improve. Very often it is just that: our body is telling us something because we have not been open to hearing it in any other way. In such cases, the physical illness or symptoms may represent symbolically the nature of the problem, as was the case with the young woman with the acne. In this way something within us forces our attention inward to where a problem of development needs our attention.

A friend of mine once had severe pains in his right shoulder. He went to several doctors for relief but no one could find anything wrong. Finally one physician said to him, "You know, those muscles of which you are complaining are exactly the muscles you would use if you wished to hit somebody." "So *that's* it," my friend thought to himself, and he proceeded to look into his hostility and the anger he had toward several people in his life. His physical symptoms vanished.

These are fairly obvious examples, but other cases are not as clear. Why should one person develop arthritis and another cancer? Has a particular illness been "chosen" for its symbolic value? We simply do not know the answer, but it is interesting to note the way our language connects certain psychic states with different parts of the body. We say, for instance, that someone gives us a "pain in the neck," or that someone is "choking with rage." We say, "I was heartsick with worry," or that somebody "lost heart," and we say, "I just could not stomach that," or "that is hard to digest." If we spend time with someone who irritates us, we might say, "That person gives me a headache," or if something affects us deeply we comment, "It got me in the gut." Of a person who makes it a point not to understand what others are saying we comment, "He turns a deaf ear." If we are anxious to act but cannot, we say, "I was itching to do something." About fear we might comment, "I was breathless with fear," or "I was scared shitless."

When we see cases in which a physical illness seems to be closely connected to a psychological state, we are tempted to say that *all* cases of physical illness are signs of a psychological or spiritual disorder. There is even a subtle temptation, as we saw before, to pass judgment on people who are ill, to become like Job's friends and say, if only to ourselves, "Well, if you would only live right (or have the right faith, or live more consciously) this wouldn't happen to you." The fact is that no one knows with what problems another person is dealing, and what fate another person has to work out in this life. Until we have stood in someone else's shoes, we had better not adopt an air of spiritual superiority, but be grateful for our own relatively good fortune.

Moreover, we cannot say that every case of illness is connected to a psychological state. Plants and animals also become diseased and no one thinks of psychosomatic factors with regard to them. Disease and illness are archetypal. They are part of the life process and will occur wherever life occurs. There is reason to believe that in some cases an illness is a necessary part of a person's development. It may be that until he has been ill in some way, that person will not achieve his maximum possible development.

There is a parable of Jesus that hints at this mysterious connection between having an illness or being injured, and becoming whole:

"There was a man who gave a great banquet, and he invited a large number of people. When the time for the banquet came, he sent his servant to say to those who had been invited, 'Come along; everything is ready now.' But all alike started to make excuses. The first said, 'I have bought a piece of land and must go and see it. Please accept my apologies.' Another said, 'I have bought five yoke of oxen and am on my way to try them out. Please accept my apologies.' Yet another said, 'I have just got married and so am unable to come.'

"The servant returned and reported this to his master. Then the householder, in a rage, said to his servant, 'Go out quickly into the streets and alleys of the town and bring in here the poor, the crippled, the blind and the lame.' 'Sir,' said the servant, 'your orders have been carried out and there is still room.' Then the master said to his servant, 'Go to the open roads and the hedgerows and force people to come in to make sure my house is full; because, I tell you, not one of those who were invited shall have a taste of my banquet.' " (Luke 14:16-24)

The banquet, as I have shown in my book on Jesus' sayings, *The Kingdom Within*, is a symbol for wholeness. The invitation is extended to all, but only those who are injured wind up accepting the invitation. Individuation always means being healed of something, but we cannot be healed unless we have been forced to recognize where we are injured or wounded. Sometimes an illness, psychological or physical, proves upon closer scrutiny to be an invitation to become a whole person, and often such illnesses can be cured only when seen in that light.

The individuation process is usually quite painful. It requires learning much about ourselves we would prefer not to know, and assuming the burden of our inner conflicts. Becoming whole is a dark and dangerous passage and it is small wonder that most people avoid it if they can. Those who do enter into individuation experience a certain woundedness. They can no longer live with illusions, and they can no longer live without letting into consciousness whatever it is that the unconscious wants to bring. Individuation is in itself a kind of wound, and there is a connection between becoming whole and experiencing one's illness and woundedness. We can even speak of individuation as a "divine wound."

In fact, we are all of us wounded people. There is no such thing as a person who is free from illness, incompleteness, and injury to his or her personality. Some of us can simply hide from our woundedness better than others. When we can no longer hide from our woundedness, we are ready for individuation. Sometimes, as already mentioned, when we think we can hide, our woundedness may go into the body to create distressing physical symptoms.

We are reminded of Chiron's wound. Chiron, a figure of Greek mythology, was a centaur who was himself skilled in healing. Unfortunately he ran afoul of Hercules and was wounded by one of his poisoned arrows. The wound proved incurable, and the only relief could come through death, but Chiron was not allowed to die. A solution finally came through the plight of Prometheus, the Titan who was being cruelly punished by Zeus for stealing fire and giving it to mankind. Chiron volunteered to go to Hades in Prometheus' place. In this way Chiron was allowed to die, and Prometheus was permitted to go free. Later Chiron was taken from Hades and made an immortal, a fitting reward for the long-suffering and compassionate physician.

The "Chironian wound" is the wound that will not heal. Those who have to work out their fate with the unconscious often feel as though they have incurred such a wound. They must continually seek God's will and grace for their lives in order to keep on living. Individuation or, if you prefer, the spiritual life, becomes a condition of life for them. They are as dependent upon gaining continual healing for their wounds as the alcoholic is upon alcohol. But this wound does not cripple them as long as it is ministered to. Instead, the continual healing of the Chironian wound results in a continued development and enlargement of personality. However, should there be an attempt to regress to a lower level of consciousness and a less meaningful way of living, the old wound would come back with vengeance, and, perhaps, create a permanent disability.

St. Paul speaks of such a Chironian wound in his famous passage on his thorn in the flesh. "I was given a thorn in the flesh," he writes the Corinthians, "an angel of Satan to beat me and stop me from getting too proud!" (II Cor. 12:7-9). We do not know what this "thorn in the flesh" was; evidently it was some type of recurring illness. Malaria has been considered, though there is a reference in the Epistle to the Galatians hinting that it might have been some kind of recurring visual disturbance, perhaps an aftermath of the blindness that struck him on the Road to Damascus. "About this thing," Paul continues, "I have pleaded with the Lord three times for it to leave me, but he has said, 'My grace is enough for you: my power is at its best in weakness.' " So Paul was never cured of this wound. Though he was a healer and healed others, he could find no relief for himself; yet it was through this wound that God's strength flowed into him. So it is that we cannot be sure what the intent or purpose of an illness is. Is the distressing symptom the result of an individuation process that has been denied? Or is it a wound through which pours a continual healing power? Each case of illness is unique, and will have a particular meaning for each person. Sweeping judgments are not possible.

The classic case of a divine wound is found in the story of Jacob and his adversary, which we find in the 32nd chapter of Genesis. In this tale, Jacob is returning to the land of Canaan to meet his estranged brother, Esau. It will be remembered that Jacob had fled from Canaan many years earlier because he had cheated his brother out of his birthright, and had stolen from him his blind father's blessing. Esau, enraged, had vowed to murder him, and Jacob had fled in fear. Now, acting under the command of God, Jacob is returning to face Esau and the consequences of his own actions many years before.

Jacob has come to the stream Jabbok, at the border of Canaan, and sent his family, servants, and flocks on ahead of him. He is alone as night falls, which is meaningful, for certain experiences come to us only when we are alone. In solitude the threshold of consciousness is lower, and contents from the unconscious can more readily cross over into consciousness. As Jacob waits, we are told, "There was one that wrestled with him until daybreak." The Hebrew word has been variously translated as "one" (Jerusalem Bible), "a man" (KJV and most other versions), "someone" (Douay Bible), or "some man" (New American Bible). Evidently it was a spiritual entity or being; we might call it a personification of the Self, the whole man.

All night the wrestling match goes on, like a struggle between Jacob and his deepest, innermost Self. Jacob's great ego strength is shown in the fact that his adversary "could not master him." Yet at the same time this divine opponent seems to have ultimate power over Jacob for we are told that he "struck him in the socket of his hip, and Jacob's hip was dislocated as he wrestled with him." Then the adversary says to Jacob, "Let me go, for day is breaking." Clearly he is a night spirit, an appearance of the unconscious that comes to us only at those times when our usual daylight consciousness has given way to the less visible things of the unconscious. But Jacob says, "I will not let you go unless you bless me." This is the courageous insistence of an ego who has suffered greatly at the hands of God, but will not give up the struggle without getting His blessing, that is, finding its meaning. The blessing is granted in the form of a change of name. Instead of the name "Jacob," which means "a supplanter," he is now known as "Israel," which means a "wrestler with God." "Because you have been strong against God," the divine adversary says to him. The change in name indicates the change in the essence of Jacob-Israel's personality. Then we are told that Jacob commented, "I have seen God face to face, and I have survived," and that the sun rose as he left, limping because of his hip.

Here is the wounding of the ego by the Self. A deep encounter with the unconscious results in a wound through which pours the life and energy of the unconscious. Jacob's injured hip represents this divine wound that he now carries as a result of his encounter with God. But it is not a neurotic, crippling wound as long as the ego ministers to it by becoming conscious of what is wanted from within.

People who are wounded in this way are fated to have to deal continually with the inner life. They may need to search out the meaning of their dreams every day, or make prayer, meditation, or other forms of self-healing a necessary part of their lives. They cannot function in life the way people do who have not been wounded by the divine forces within them. If such a person turns his back upon his wounds, he becomes ill again; the wound festers once more and poisons him. But as long as the wound is ministered to, it proves a source of renewal and life. It becomes an opening through which new life enters into and enlarges consciousness. It is the divine wound.

Just as there seems to be a relationship between illness and individuation, there also seems to be a relationship between individuation and death. Death, for instance, may come when the path to individuation is blocked. Suicide is a special instance of this. The causes of suicide are manifold, but its symbolic nature should not be overlooked. With many people who commit suicide it is as though something in them is telling them that they must do it. This is a symbolic expression of the fact that there are attitudes in the conscious personality that are standing in the way of wholeness and these attitudes must be "killed," that is, removed, gotten out of the way. If the movement toward individuation is unconscious, the suicidal impulse may be acted out. Such suicides could be averted if the person were able to see the symbolic meaning of his suicidal fantasies, namely, that a faulty state of consciousness must be put to death and a new state of being emerge.

In cases of "natural" death the relationship of the individual to his or her individuation may also be the root of the matter. When further development in life is impossible, a process of dying may begin. Life will not stand still. It either develops further, or begins to move toward death. Individuation might become impossible when an individual is either unconscious of his inner dynamics and the meaning of his life, or when he finds himself in a life situation that is an impasse.

An example of a life that reached an impasse and then suddenly ended is that of General George Patton. Patton was the total soldier. A biographer wrote of him, "This seems to me the record of a man who was devoted to war."[7] In fact, when in North Africa, he believed that he had fought earlier wars there in previous existences. He identified with "Ares," the god of war, or, as we would say today, he identified with an archetype. As a soldier he was magnificent, and his energy for the war amounted to a passion. Amazingly, he went through four years of World War II, in which he often shared the hardships and dangers with his men, unscathed, but a few months after the cessation of hostilities Patton was killed in an accident. Could it be that the spirit of this man who was so identical with warmaking could find no way to continue living in a time of peace? We will never know the answer, but the possibility exists that this was the case. It would be an illustration of the way death can be constellated in an individual when there is no longer any place for the life energy to go.

We usually think of death as physical, of course, but there is also such a thing as spiritual death. Some people go on living a vegetable-like existence, but it is as though their souls are no longer with them. Life lingers on and on, but it has become meaningless and the person is for all spiritual intents and purposes already dead. Perhaps there is such a thing as the spirit's leaving the personality even though the shell of the body remains, though ordinarily we think of death as resulting when the spirit and the body separate.

If death may come when individuation is blocked, it may also come when individuation has been fulfilled. Perhaps we die when we have reached the maximum amount of development possible for us in this life.

The life of C. G. Jung gives us an interesting example. In his 70th year Jung suffered a severe heart attack that almost resulted in his death. As he lingered at the door of death, Jung experienced a great vision. He seemed to be taken high up into space until he came to an illuminated room like a great temple. As he approached this he understood that when he entered he would at last understand the meaning of his life. The experience was different from an ordinary vision. It was not as though it was something he was "seeing," but something he was experiencing, an actual journey through another mode of reality. But just as he was about to enter the illuminated temple he saw the form of his doctor coming toward him. "As he stood before me," Jung wrote in his autobiography, "a mute exchange of thought took place between us. Dr. H. had been delegated by the earth to deliver a message to me, to tell me that there was a protest against my going away. I had no right to leave the earth and must return. The moment I heard that, the vision ceased. I was profoundly disappointed, for now it all seemed to have been for nothing. The painful process of defoliation had been in vain, and I was not to be allowed to enter the temple, to join the people in whose company I belonged. In reality, a good three weeks were still to pass before I could truly make up my mind to live again. I could not eat because all food repelled me. The view of city and mountains from my sickbed seemed to me like a painted curtain with black holes in it, or a tattered sheet of newspaper full of photographs that meant nothing. Disappointed I thought, 'Now I must return to the "box system" again.' "[8]

Jung recovered and lived another seventeen years. During this last phase of his life he wrote his most important works, and reached his greatest stature as a man. He was never more impressive than in his old age. Had he died at the age of 70 he would not have reached the culmination of his development, and the world would have been impoverished by the loss of his most important writings. He continued writing until a few days before his death at the age of 87. I am told that in his last few days, as he lingered between life and death once again, Jung spoke again of overwhelmingly beautiful visions. At last he died, for now his life had been fulfilled. Perhaps he was then allowed to enter the great illuminated temple.

Sometimes dreams come prior to death suggesting that the portending death is indeed the fulfillment of life. Such a dream came to my father, who had a long illness before his death at the age of 71. He was not a man who was used to recording his dreams, but this dream, which came a week prior to his death, made a great impact upon him so that he told it to my mother. The dream is given in her words. The meaning of the dream, that it spoke of his imminent death, was clear to them both.

> "In the dream he awakened in his living room. But then the room changed and he was back in his room in the old house in Vermont as a child. Again the room changed: to Connecticut (where he had his first job), to China (where he had lived many years), to Pennsylvania, to New Jersey (where he had been a minister for 22 years), and then back to the living room. In each scene after China, I [my mother] was present, in each instance being of a different age in accordance with the time represented. Finally he sees himself lying on the couch back in the living room. I am descending the stairs and the doctor is in the room. The doctor says, 'Oh, he's gone.' Then, as the others fade in the dream, he sees the clock on the mantelpiece; the hands have been moving, but now they stop; as they stop, a window opens behind the mantelpiece clock and a bright light shines through. The opening widens into a door and the light becomes a brilliant path. He walks out on the path of light and disappears."

What happens if death comes before a person has fulfilled his purpose on this earth? We cannot answer this question, of course. Yet when one follows the course of a person's inner life one often gets the impression that we are here on this earth for the purpose of developing and purifying the life of the soul; in psychological language, for the purpose of individuation. Perhaps, as Jung hinted, this earthly life is a "box system" specially set up for us, an experience of finitude and limitation that is necessary for a certain development to take place. If we run our course in this life, and our development on this earth is completed, death may come as release and fulfillment. The moment of death may even be timed to coincide with the moment of the most completed development. If we perish without having achieved our purpose, perhaps we must run the race again, either in this life or some mode of existence to come.

If death may come when a person has reached fulfillment in this life, and if further development now lies beyond this world, then we might assume it would be wrong to interfere with a natural process intended to bring about the transition. What happens, then, when a person who is ready to die is not allowed to die because of radical medical intervention?

A woman in her late seventies consulted me because of a series of six puzzling dreams that came to her during an acute illness. This woman had been saved from certain death by two heroic operations, and the faithful and skillful intervention of a team of dedicated doctors and nurses. For three weeks she had lingered at the door of death in the intensive care unit of the hospital until finally she was saved by the great skill of modern medical treatment.

On a conscious level she could not say enough in the way of gratitude and admiration for the help she had received, but her dreams suggested a different story. Each dream took place in the intensive care unit of the hospital, and in most of them she was angry and indignant. Her attitude in the dreams was the exact opposite of her conscious attitude. Not enough is known of the dreamer's associations to the dreams to be clear about their meaning. It may be that her anger expressed her frustration at her helplessness in the situation. But it is also possible that her spirit, expressed through her dreams, was opposed to her recovery, and that she felt cheated of the right to die.

> "Again we have been on the move," she dreams. "I have been led to believe that I am being taken to my son. I am told that we are within two hours' drive of his house. But the nurses won't take me there. For the first time in the dream sequence I become *very* angry. 'You promised me, you promised me you would take me to my son,' I can hear myself crying in anguished, despairing sobbing. This is when I first felt that I had been betrayed and kidnapped."

In another dream she relates,

> "I have been taken to a room—sort of a show room. I'm no longer in the coffin-like bed but sort of on display in a hospital bed. I can hear footsteps of many people outside walk-

ing on what seems to be the streets of Los Angeles. My feelings have changed from uncontrollable anger to a sort of helpless despair—powerless to help myself and at the mercy of my attendants. Behind the room I am in is another show room where all kinds of instruments and gadgets are on display and people from the street are coming in to view them and be told how these will cure their illnesses. I'm indignant and feel that they are being misled and being sold a bill of goods—that these gadgets won't cure them at all."

When we seek to relate wholeness to illness and health, life and death, we wind up with more questions than answers. Sweeping statements become impossible. We cannot say, "All illness is a case of an individuation process that has been missed," for there also seem to be cases in which an illness is an important part of a person's individuation, that a certain stage of development could not have been achieved without it. We will look at more examples of this when we study shamanism, where it is clear that for certain people, at certain times in their lives, the way toward wholeness requires an experience of illness. There is also the strange fact that the process leading toward wholeness is in itself a kind of wound. Yet at the same time there are other cases in which it seems clear that a life-bringing process that has been initiated by the unconscious, then blocked or denied, has resulted in a disorder in the body. Every case of illness must be considered on its own merit. No one should be too quick to judge or evaluate the illness of another person until he is in possession of many facts about that person's soul. The one thing that is fairly clear is that there *is* a connection between individuation and physical health, a connection that may even determine the moment of death. How do we come into contact with those forces that can make us whole? The Greeks, as usual, had something to say about this, and it is to this that we now turn as we study the life and cult of the Greek god of healing, Asklepius.

Notes

1. This attitude toward illness dies a hard death. Consider, e.g., this prayer for the Visitation of the Sick found in the 1928 Book of Common Prayer, p. 313, which was the official Prayer Book in use in the Episcopal Church until 1977:
"O most merficul God, who, according to the multitude of thy mercies,

dost so put away the sins of those who truly repent, that thou remem-
berest them no more; Open thine eye of mercy upon this thy servant,
who most earnestly desireth pardon and forgiveness. Renew in him,
most loving Father, whatsoever hath been decayed by the fraud and mal-
ice of the devil, or by his own carnal will and frailness; preserve and continue this sick member in the unity of the Church; consider his contri-
tion, accept his tears, assuage his pain, as shall seem to thee most
expedient for him. And forasmuch as he putteth his full trust only in thy
mercy, impute not unto him his former sins, but strengthen him with thy
blessed Spirit. . . ."
I am happy to say that in the revised Prayer Book of 1977 the Episcopal
Church has deleted this prayer, and has a new order for the Visitation of the
Sick that is free from the implication that sickness is the direct result of sin.

2. Cf. the September 1974, *National Geographic*, p. 426ff.

3. Flanders Dunbar, *Mind and Body; Psychosomatic Medicine* (New
York: Random House, 1955), chapter 8.

4. Cf. Barbara Hannah in *Jung, His Life and Work* (New York: G. P.
Putnam's Sons, 1976), p. 63. Also, C.G. Jung, *Letters* (Princeton, N.J.:
Princeton University Press), Vol. II, p. 297, the letter to Rudolf Jung.

5. C.G. Jung, *Letters* (Princeton, N.J.: Princeton University Press), Vol.
II, p. 58.

6. See the very interesting correspondence between C.G. Jung and Wil-
liam in the January 1968 *Grapevine* magazine, a publication of Alcoholics
Anonymous. Jung and William are discussing the other co-founder of A.A.,
Roland, who, in 1931, consulted with Jung for a year prior to founding A.A.
In 1961 Jung still remembered his conversations with Roland and wrote:
"His craving for alcohol was the equivalent, on a low level, of the spiritual
thirst of our being for wholeness, expressed in medieval language: the union
with God."

7. H. Essame, *Patton: A Study in Command* (New York: Charles
Scribner's Sons, 1974), Prologue. He is quoting from Xenophon of Clearous,
the Spartan General c. 360 B.C., and applying this quotation to Patton as
well.

8. C.G. Jung, *Memories, Dreams, Reflections* (Pantheon Books, 1961),
Chapter 10.

meaning is central, in sickness and health. Stages of meaning, its loss and rediscovery, after a crisis/expansion. Each new inclusive. Sometimes disease is the teacher

III

The Divine Physician

In the ancient world of Greece and Rome, there was something unique: an institution dedicated to healing. Complete with a mythology, symbolism, temples, priesthood, and method of healing, the cult of Asklepius has much to tell us of the mystery of healing.

Asklepius' story begins with the love affair between Apollo, Greek god of music, harmony, the movement of the sun, and also a sender of both disease and healing, and the mortal woman Coronis. Apollo, enamored of Coronis, made her his mistress, and as a result of their union she became pregnant. Being a god, it was not Apollo's way to linger long in the bonds of marital fidelity, and so he soon left his mortal love and resumed his godlike activities. He had, however, a double standard, one for himself and one for Coronis, for he expected his mortal wife to remain faithful to him even though he was not faithful to her. Suspecting she might not be able or willing to do this, Apollo sent a bird—the crow—to watch over her and report to him what she did. In those days crows were white. Sure enough, Coronis tired of waiting for Apollo to return and took Ischys, a mortal, for her lover, and the crow dutifully flew back to Apollo and reported the treachery. The enraged Apollo turned the crow black to express his anger, and then plotted his revenge. Coronis was to discover that it was a dangerous thing to be made love to by a god, even as today it is a dangerous thing for a man or woman to be sought out for union by those mysterious, enormous powers that lie within the unconscious.

Apollo's revenge was swift and merciless. The hapless Coronis was slain and her body placed upon a funeral pyre. The flames were just beginning to lick away at her body when Apollo, somewhat as an afterthought, remembered the unborn child. Swooping down from the sky, the god ripped open Coronis's womb and drew out his premature son, who was destined to become the great physician, Asklepius.

The peculiar circumstances of Asklepius' birth give us the first clue about his inner meaning: he was "snatched from death," to use the phrase of C. A. Meier whose fine book on the cult of Asklepius is a classic in its field.[1] So it is with those who are close to the archetype

42

of healing. They live and work close to death, and they themselves, as we shall see, are people who have felt the hot breath of death or illness, and have narrowly escaped destruction.

The gods, of course, were no more inclined to child-rearing than to domestic fidelity, so Apollo did not raise his little son himself, but entrusted him instead to the centaur, Chiron. Chiron was himself a physician, gifted in healing, and steeped in medical lore. He raised the little boy in a pastoral setting, close to the earth and to animals, and as he grew he imparted to him his knowledge of healing. In time the boy became a young man following in his adoptive father's footsteps, but in addition to the knowledge he had acquired from Chiron, the young Asklepius received a special gift. Athene, impressed by his wisdom and bearing, gave him the gift of the Gorgon's blood. The Gorgon Medusa had been a terrible female monster, with snakes for hair, so dreadful that merely to look upon her turned the bravest man to stone. She had been destroyed by the Greek hero Perseus, with the aid of Athene and Hermes, and her blood had been caught and kept all these years. It seemed that the blood that flowed from the left side of Medusa brought death, and the blood that flowed from the right side brought healing. The paradoxical quality of this blood reflects the closeness between illness and health, and points to the equally paradoxical quality of the unconscious that both wounds and heals.

Equipped with the Gorgon's blood and the medical skill of Chiron, Asklepius became a highly successful physician. He moved about among the people healing the sick and injured wherever he went, and it was said that even the dead were called back to life. Mankind rejoiced in their healer and loved him greatly. But unfortunately for human suffering, Asklepius' very success brought down upon him the wrath and enmity of Hades, King of the Underworld, who complained to Zeus that the population of his kingdom was being depleted because of Asklepius, and that he, Hades, was being cheated of what was rightfully his. Zeus took Hades' side in the matter and slew Asklepius with a thunderbolt. Then there was heard a terrible cry of anguish because mankind's saviour and healer had been destroyed. So great was the agony that Zeus was moved to mercy, and at last, with the consent of the gods, Asklepius was raised from the dead and placed among the immortals. In this way Asklepius, who began as a human physician, became a divine healer. Once again Asklepius had been to the door of death and then returned to life.

In Greek art and tradition, Asklepius was closely associated with his family, and with various theriomorphic representations. His wife was Epione, who was noted for the soothing quality in her gentle hands. This reminds us of the healing property long associated with the hands. Hands symbolize an instrument of power, and energy is said to flow through them. From ancient times prayer for the sick has been administered in the rite of the "laying on of hands," and any parent knows how instinctive it is to lay a soothing hand upon the brow of a sick child.

Asklepius' daughters are even more important and have familiar names: Iaso, Panacea, and Hygeia. From their names we have our English words "panacea," a cure-all, and "hygiene," which is the science of health. He also had two sons, Podaleirius and Machaon, who were also skilled physicians, and served in the Trojan War. It was Machaon who cured the stricken Menelaus of an arrow wound, although he himself was finally killed in the struggle. More important than his sons, however, was Telesphorus, the immortal boy who, like Asklepius, was a sender of dreams, and was closely associated with the god as his companion. Telesphorus seems to personify a guardian spirit for those who are ill. He was characteristically shown in a hooded cape, which was also the garment worn by those who had recovered from an illness.

The primary theriomorphic symbol for Asklepius was the serpent. In fact, Asklepius *was* the serpent, and the appearance of a serpent in a dream amounted to the appearance of the god himself. It was in snake form, for instance, that tradition says Asklepius came from Greece to Rome. Rome was suffering from a terrible plague and in her agony sent an envoy to Greece to beseech the famous god of healing to come to her aid. Asklepius consented and was transported to Rome in the form of a great serpent; a temple was established in his honor on an island in the Tiber River. Here the serpent-god took up his residence and the pestilence in Rome was conquered. The remnants of this temple can still be seen, although a Christian shrine has been erected upon it.

The close association between the serpent and Asklepius is represented in Asklepius' great symbol: the staff with a serpent entwined about it. This staff of Asklepius has become the symbol of the medical profession, although today doctors and patients alike probably recall little of the mythological origin of the serpent-staff that represents the healing arts and power.

Today we tend to associate the serpent with evil, largely because of the story about him in the Garden of Eden. Christian theologians have interpreted this story in terms of the origin of sin and evil and placed the blame for these evils on the serpent's cunning and the weakness of Adam and Eve. Ancient man, however, did not see the serpent as evil, but rather as a symbol of the renewing, transforming energy that lies at the heart of life. Even early Christian theologians did not all agree that the serpent in the Garden of Eden embodied evil. Some saw that without the serpent the whole process of salvation would never have started; others believed the serpent carried out the divine purpose of bringing consciousness to mankind, rather than introducing evil.

In almost all other mythologies than the Christian the serpent symbolizes a beneficent, if awesome, power. A good example of the way the ancients regarded the serpent is found in the Babylonian hero myth of Gilgamesh. Gilgamesh was a man of truly heroic proportions, renowned for his great strength, wisdom, and high character. The only thing Gilgamesh lacked to become one of the gods was immortality, and finally he went in search of this gift. After many trials and perils, Gilgamesh was told that in the bottom of the sea there was a certain plant the name of which meant "the-old-man-becomes-young," and if anyone would eat of this plant he would have eternal life. Gilgamesh dove to the bottom of the sea, succeeded in finding the plant of eternal life, plucked it, and returned safely. Immortality was now in his grasp and victory was won, but Gilgamesh, exhausted by his effort, decided first to rest. Soon the exhausted hero fell asleep and while he slept a serpent came. When Gilgamesh awoke, it was to see the serpent eating the last of the plant of immortality; a moment later the serpent shed his skin and stood before the horrified hero in his shining new skin. In this way, the ancients said, it happened that man remained mortal, while the power of renewal, represented in the shedding of the old skin and emergence in a new one, became the gift of the serpent.

The other significant animal representation of Asklepius was the dog. Though his dog form was less important than his serpent form, there are many ancient artistic representations of the god in which there stands beside him his faithful animal. Perhaps the ancients were drawing here upon the prevalent symbolism of the dog as a guide of souls through the regions of the underworld, for reasons we will look at shortly.

The myth of Asklepius became enshrined in an institution of healing unprecedented in history. If you were ill in ancient Greece or Rome, your first recourse probably would be to go to one of the Asklepiads, scientifically trained physicians, who had skills in diagnosis, certain kinds of surgery, and an assortment of herbs and medicines. The scientific medical lore of these ancient doctors was probably as good as any doctors until the present day. Everything they knew, so it was believed, was given to them by the direct inspiration and teaching of the great god of healing himself. But if these means of healing should fail, you might consider undertaking a journey to one of the many temples of Asklepius, perhaps one of the famous ones at Cos, Pergamon, or Epidauros. You had many to choose from, for modern archaeologists have uncovered over four hundred of them.

After you arrived at one of Asklepius' temples, you were received by the priests who were in attendance. They had a therapeutic function but were not themselves therapists, for the healing was done by the direct intervention of the god in the soul of the patient. The first task of the priests was to determine if you were a fit candidate to enter the temple. It was important that Asklepius himself had summoned you; in fact, the special place in the temple where the healing would take place was known as the *abaton*, which means "a place not to be entered into uninvited." The invitation would ordinarily be extended to you through a dream, so that we must picture the priests at the temple asking a patient about his dreams, and attempting to ascertain if the dreams contained within them an invitation from the god to visit his sacred temple. It was also important that a patient not be at the point of death, for it would be unfortunate if someone died in the temple itself (one can imagine what a bad effect this would have on others!). Pregnant women, for reasons unknown to me, also were forbidden entrance to the temple.

If it was decided that you were called to the temple, rites of purification would begin. An interview with the priest would accomplish what we would call today catharsis or confession, for it was recognized that unless a person was right with himself, and had put his life in order, he could not expect healing from the god. This purification of the soul was further accomplished by ritual bathing, both body and soul being cleansed in the healing waters of the springs or streams near which the temples were always built.

After the priests had performed their function, you were ready to go to the god himself for healing, and went to the special chamber, the abaton. In this sparsely furnished room was a couch, called in Greek the *kline,* and here you were left alone with the hope that as you slept the god would appear to you in a healing dream. It was through the dream that Asklepius would bring healing, and the days and nights spent alone in the abaton were a time of *incubation*, from a Greek word meaning "a sleeping in," in which it was hoped that the god would manifest himself.

After the incubation was accomplished and, hopefully, the sought-for dream had come, you would emerge from the abaton and go again to the priests. The dream would be reported to them and they would help determine if it was from the god. The priests did not interpret dreams, however, for the healing came, not in the interpretations, but in the dream experience itself, which was believed to be such a direct contact with the god that interpretation was not necessary.

Patients who were healed recorded the stories of their healing in plaques that were placed upon the walls of the temple. Many of these ancient witnesses to healing have been recovered; they must have made reassuring reading to the newly arrived seekers after health. Finally a fee was paid to the priests for the maintenance and work of the temple, and it was said that if the fee was not paid a relapse would occur.

The widespread institution of Asklepius and its many temples gives evidence not only to the ever-present hunger of mankind for healing but also to the efficacy of Asklepius' healing power. There must have been many people who found healing in this way, and the happy outcome of their efforts must have spurred others to undertake the journey to a temple of the god, and kept alive the hope of healing to which the cult of the god was dedicated. Perhaps we will be able to see in the myth of Asklepius, and the means of healing his temples afforded, important messages for those who would find healing today.

Asklepius, as has been mentioned, was "snatched from death." He journeyed to the very jaws of death, indeed into the underworld itself, and then returned. He is fit to be a master of the mysteries of illness and death, healing and life, because he knows them firsthand. He is a prime example of what has been called the "Wounded Healer," and a startling example of the mysterious connection between illness and health. The healing power flows, not through those who have known only health, but through those who have been ill, have been drawn near the dark land of death, and have then been healed. This is not to say that everyone who has been ill and recovered is called upon to be a healer, but it is to say that people in whom the healing power moves will be those who have come into contact with the mystery of the Wounded Healer. As we shall see in the next chapter, there appear to be certain people who are destined for illness, in order that through their illness and recovery they might be able to function as healers to needy mankind. For only through illness or a journey to the underworld can the archetype of the Wounded Healer come alive in a human being.

The fact that Asklepius received the gift of the Gorgon's blood gives him a peculiarly ambivalent function in relationship to illness. He has in his hands the power to bestow either life or death, for it is the same mysterious energy, symbolized by the blood of the Gorgon, that can give either one. It is a strange fact that the source of healing energy is often represented as also being the source of illness and death. It is said of Apollo, for instance, Asklepius' father and himself a healing god, that he is the "one who wounds and also heals." In the Old Testament we also read of Yahweh: "For he who wounds is he who soothes the sore, and the hand that hurts is the hand that heals." (Job 5:18)

This seemingly peculiar fact is explained by the unusual quality of the unconscious, for the unconscious is a source of illness *and* a source of healing. When consciousness is affected in a certain way by the contents of the unconscious, an illness may well result; in fact, the first contact with the unconscious almost always results in an illness because of the disturbance it brings to consciousness. We can, for instance, be taken over by a figure or content of the unconscious. In such cases of psychological possession, the result is a darkening of consciousness with a resulting disturbance in our lives and our relationships. The most frequent cases of this sort occur when a man is possessed by his unrecognized feminine side, and a woman by her unrecognized masculine side. There are also times when the ego is overwhelmed by the unconscious. Such cases result in disorientation, depression, or even psychosis, or, if the ego instinctively fights against being overwhelmed, by a violent, uncontrollable anxiety. A person in such a state may dream of being down in the bottom of the ocean, or of gigantic waves breaking over him. It is like being swallowed up in the belly of a monster and the effect can be so overwhelming that a person is crippled or incapacitated until the experience has been understood and integrated.

Yet this same unconscious power, which can so painfully affect and disturb our conscious functioning, can also be the healing power. If the ego can discriminate what is happening, come into relationship with the unconscious contents, and begin to see what is wanted of it, the illness can be reversed and healing can begin to take place. It is as though the unconscious does not *want* to possess or overwhelm consciousness, but wants relationship or union with the ego. The first attempt to bring this about, however, results not in union, but in an unfortunate *mixing* of the conscious and the unconscious minds, because the ego is unprepared for the experience and does not understand it. This is the darkening of consciousness the ancient alchemists called the *nigredo*, the feared and dreaded *melancholia*, but it was recognized by them to be an essential step in the alchemical process. It is the attitude and understanding of consciousness that makes the difference. With the correct attitude, and the proper understanding of what is happening, the true intentions of the unconscious are revealed, and what began as an illness eventually becomes a healing and transforming experience. In a later chapter we will look more closely at the way this works.

It is a significant part of the myth that Asklepius is the source of both natural or scientific healing, and charismatic or spiritual healing. The scientific medicine of the day, as we saw, believed its knowledge and inspiration came from the god. In our present day we have an unfortunate division between the scientific and spiritual sides of healing. The scientific knowledge of medicine has developed enormously since the days of the ancient Asklepiads, but without a proper recognition of the spiritual foundation of both illness and health, the results remain questionable. There are those patients, as we have suggested in the previous chapter, whose illness is of spiritual and not physical origin, and who must be treated spiritually and psychologically as well as physically if ultimate healing is to take place. There are also many people who cannot or will not be healed unless they come into contact with a transforming energy that can renew the lives of their souls as well as the lives of their bodies, and there will always be the people whose illness cannot be touched by medicines, surgery, or drugs, and who must, if they are to become whole again, go to the source of healing itself.

Even scientific medical lore, as the ancient Greeks knew, is a gift from the gods. True knowledge, in science as well as in the arts, is a matter of inspiration. We do not think up knowledge, it *comes to us*. Without detracting for a moment from the important work of the ego in testing and assimilating knowledge, it nevertheless remains a fact that creative advances in science are also a gift from God. The German language recognizes this in its word *Einfall*, which is what we could call an "idea." An idea is, for the Germans, a "falling-in," something which *falls into one's head*. This is a verbal testimony to the understanding the ancient Greek healing cult recognized, that both scientific knowledge and charismatic healing have one source.

Although Asklepius had two sons, as mentioned earlier, the most important figures who surround him are the feminine members of his family; they are the ones to whom, along with Asklepius himself, petitions of prayer might be addressed. The reason for the importance of these feminine figures lies in the necessity for the inclusion of the

feminine principle if healing is to take place. The feminine principle—
of eros, relatedness, and nature—is an essential ingredient of a spiritual or psychological healing process. Every psychological or spiritual
counselor knows this, for it is clear that without a relationship between counselor and client, and without the feminine powers of
warmth, concern, and intuitive understanding, the healing process will
not work. Most important, the soul herself, which is always feminine,
must be present if healing is to occur.

A contrast with the Old Testament may make this clear. It is a
remarkable fact that in the Old Testament there is practically no
healing, and virtually no healers in the entire Old Testament drama.
It is true that there are isolated healing stories, such as Elisha's cure
of Naaman the Syrian and Elijah's restoration to life of the widow's
son, but these are rare exceptions. As for Yahweh, occasionally He
heeds the pleas of His people and sends healing to them, for instance
when He instructed Moses to make a brazen serpent and hold it up so
the people of Israel who had been bitten by snakes would be cured,
but generally He is not interested in healing. It is not healing, but the
obedience of His people to Him and later the requirements of social
justice, that He demands, and His servants are not healers, but
prophets and reformers.

The paucity of healing in the Old Testament is graphically illus-
trated in the story of Saul. The King has become ill with a deep
depressive state with paranoid tendencies. His courtiers ascribe the
source of this malady to Yahweh Himself. "Look," they say to Saul,
"an evil spirit of God is the cause of your terror." One would suppose
that at this point they might call for a physician or shaman, but instead they say, "Let our lord give the order, and your servants who
wait on you will look for a skilled harpist; when the evil spirit of God
troubles you, the harpist will play and you will recover." (I Samuel
16:15-16) It was in this way that David first came to Saul's court,
and his ability as a harpist and musician did cure Saul of his depressive moods, but only temporarily, and soon they returned darker than
ever. It is known that in ancient Greece music was regarded as having
healing properties, but music in itself is not enough. Evidently a
musician was called to Saul's court by the King's concerned courtiers
because either there were no physicians or healers, or there was no
faith in them. The fact is, there is no specific mention of a physician
or healer in the entire Old Testament, and only a few general references to physicians, at least one of which casts aspersions upon the
profession.[2]

This is strange, for we find the profession of the healer to be exceedingly ancient; the most primitive peoples had their healers, as we will see in the next chapter. It is the more remarkable since the New Testament is filled with healing, and Jesus is a healer par excellence. Wherever he goes the sick are healed, the crippled walk again, the mentally afflicted recover, and later we learn that his disciples were healers as well. The difference seems to be the inclusion in the New Testament of a feminine element that was missing in the one-sidedly masculine Yahweh. In the Old Testament God is a fiercely masculine being, Who is wildly jealous of the fertility goddess Astarte, who is the goddess of the Canaanites, and forbids His people to have anything to do with her feminine rituals. With rare exceptions, there is no feminine element or quality in the fierce and demanding Yahweh. But in the New Testament we are told that the Saviour is born of the union of the Holy Spirit with Mary. It is as though the feminine element is introduced by the inclusion of Mary in the story, and the figure of the Saviour, Jesus, is of a man who is very close to the feminine influence. This is shown not only in his qualities of intuition, concern for people, and relatedness, but in the close association Jesus had with many women (Mary and Martha, Mary Magdalene, the woman by the well of Samaria, etc.), which was an extraordinary thing for that highly patriarchal era. The lack of healing in the Old Testament, and the profusion of healing in the New Testament, can therefore be accounted for on the basis of the inclusion of the feminine element in the latter narratives.

In addition to his daughters, another feminine influence in Asklepius' story is the importance of water. As we have seen, his temples were established near, or over, sources of water, usually natural springs. Patients who came for healing, we noted, had to undergo ritual purification in this water. Water has a feminine significance. It is like a container of life, a womb from which life springs and in which it is nourished. Life began in the waters of the ocean, and it is certainly true that neither plant nor animal life can exist without this essential element. In our dreams we will find that water is the most common symbol for the unconscious, and often refers to the life-giving qualities of the soul. The importance of water in Asklepius' cult suggests that healing is not possible without some kind of contact with the inner waters of the soul, the water that Jesus says becomes a spring welling up to eternal life (John 4:14).

The symbolism of the serpent, as we saw in the story of Gilgamesh, is connected to the ancient association of the serpent with the power to renew its own life. Life has a self-renewing energy. Plants, in dying, renew their own kind by the profusion of seeds they leave. Parents, in a way, die in the lives of their children. Even cells of the body die and are replaced by new cells, so that the physical organism of man must be thought of as constantly renewing itself. The life of the soul also must constantly be renewed. Energy is born, is used, dies, and is reborn within us over and over again. The ego is dependent on the renewal of life and energy from within. Cut off from inner life-giving sources, the life of consciousness atrophies and dies. The serpent-power of the unconscious, the strange, primitive, vital energy of those archetypal sources of life, must be contacted if healing and renewal are to occur.

A strange event occurred in my ministry some years ago that illustrates the enduring symbol of the serpent as a healing power. A young woman in my congregation called me one day in great anguish. Her five-year-old son had been stricken with spinal meningitis and was acutely ill in the contagious diseases section of the Los Angeles County Hospital. She was requesting the prayers of the congregation, and of course prayers were said for her and her son. Early the next morning she called me again, terrified because of the following dream that had come to her during the night:

> "My husband and I were outside, looking into the room where my son was asleep. I saw to my horror a great snake on the floor, crawling toward the boy, and cried out to my husband to go in the room and stop him. But the snake reached the boy first, and bit him on the forehead between the eyes. My husband emerged with the boy, bleeding slightly, and I was terrified. I awoke, certain he would now die."

In fact, her son did not die but began to recover that very day; eventually he made a total recovery from his illness, though the other two boys in the same room with him suffered brain damage. To this woman, with her Christian prejudices against the snake, the dream was threatening, but had the dream come to an ancient Greek it would have been greeted with joy, for the snake would have been recognized as Asklepius himself who had come to heal the child.

Although somewhat less important than the symbolism of the serpent, the dog as a symbol for Asklepius was also significant. The symbol in mythology of the dog as a guide has already been noted. Anyone who has had a hunting or sporting type of dog is aware that the dog possesses senses and instincts human beings lack. My own dog, for instance, while ordinarily quite friendly, has certain people to whom he has a distinct aversion. He has his own reasons for his intense dislike of these people and no amount of reasoning on my part can persuade him to change his mind. My dog also perceives things I do not perceive. If we wander together in the country, he will send a score of rabbits and birds I had not seen flying from cover as his keen nose searches out things hidden from my eyes. A dog, of course, proceeds upon instinct, not upon reason, but his instinct is a sure guide. No matter how far he wanders from me, my dog always knows how to find his way back, and there are, of course, fascinating stories of dogs who have been lost for a long time eventually returning to their masters.

It may be that the dog is so important in Asklepius' symbolism because of the great importance of instinct in the healing process. To find our healing, we must be guided by our instinct, as well as by our reason; in fact instinct is the surer guide of the two. Instinct is especially important in selecting a person to help us find healing. If we let our inner dog sniff out a doctor or counselor for us, we are much more likely to find the correct person for our needs than if we trust our rational side. The "dog" within us makes himself felt by an instinctive response that says "yes" or "no" to the healing resources that are offered to us. Often such responses cannot be given rational formulation, but they need to be followed.

The inner dog may also manifest his instinct for finding the right path in the images and fantasies that cross our minds and that, if followed, may heal us. Sometimes if we are distraught we may find a fantasy suddenly chasing itself through our consciousness; perhaps we see ourselves swimming, or walking through the mountains, or working in the garden. This may be our inner dog telling us through instinct what it is we need to do to heal ourselves.

Occasionally my inner dog operates within me for the benefit of other people. I recall one man who came to me very depressed, with a chronic skin irritation no medicine seemed able to cure. Suddenly there came into my consciousness a scene of this man immersed in the ocean. I shared my fantasy with him for what it was worth. Later I learned from him that he had left my office and had gone directly to the ocean where he spent two hours bathing in the salt water. By the next day his depression was gone and his skin irritation also had disappeared.

Salt water seems to have unusual healing properties. Another man of my acquaintance had to give a musical performance in the evening, but to his great distress found himself virtually paralyzed that day by a crippling depression brought on by some disturbing events of the day. He was so devoid of energy that he could scarcely function, and the thought of the public performance he was expected to make that evening was crushing him with despair. Instinctively he went to the sea, and soon, hardly thinking about it, he found himself wading into the ocean fully clothed until the waters reached up over his chest. Here he remained for a long time and it was as though the swirling salt waters washed the darkness out of him and replaced his sagging spirits with energy. Almost miraculously cured, he emerged from the sea a new man and performed that evening more capably than ever before. We could say that he had followed his "dog" who somehow knew what he must do to cure himself.

A woman once came to me for help with her anger. Absolutely nothing seemed to be able to free her from the grip of a dark rage that was possessing her and draining all her life energy. I had exhausted my resources in helping her understand and deal with this anger and nothing had worked. I had. nothing more to offer and she left my office disconsolate and disappointed. When she returned the following week, however, she told me that her anger had disappeared that very day. She had returned home terribly upset and somehow, without quite knowing why, had wound up ironing clothes (something she hardly ever did herself). "It was as though the steam from the iron steamed away my anger," she related. I have had the same experience weeding the garden, but it would never have occurred to me to suggest to this woman that she iron clothes so that the steam could dissipate her anger. In this case it was her inner dog that led her to the right action.

The symbolism surrounding the cult of Asklepius is rich with the lore and wisdom of healing, and the patient who went to the healing shrine was immersed in this fruitful and creative imagery. Indeed, from the moment the patient conceived the notion of seeking healing from the god to the very end of his journey, he was in touch with healing forces. His journey began with a recognition of need, an acknowledgment that he had to seek help from a source beyond himself. Without this no spiritual or psychological healing is possible. The patient stopped seeing the causes of his distress in others, or in outer circumstances, and acknowledged that his illness was a part of himself and that he needed renewal. As we saw in the first chapter, no illness is more dangerous than an illness that a person does not admit belongs to him, for in that case the pain of the malfunctioning is felt by others and a cure is impossible.

The second step the patient took was to pay attention to his dreams in the hope that a dream would come that was an invitation by the god to visit his sanctuary. In this way the individual looked to

self healing

his own soul for help and therefore had an opportunity to come into contact with his own healing forces. This is exceedingly important, for every organism is self-healing, and the psyche as well as the body contains within itself a healing center, as we will see in a later chapter.

A certain amount of creative introversion is an essential part of healing. If we are ill with the flu, our instinct is to find a quiet place, rest, seclude ourselves, shut out the world, and let the healing powers of the body make us whole again. The healing of the soul also requires introversion, for only in this state can a certain kind of centering take place. To aid themselves in this process of introverted centering, many people keep a Journal in which they record their dreams, fears, fantasies, inspired thoughts or whatever it is that makes up the uninvited stream of thoughts and images that cross into consciousness from the unconscious. Perhaps the supplicant at the shrine of Asklepius kept such a Journal. At least, as soon as he began to look into his dreams he was keeping in touch with the stream of life from within, making a deliberate journey, as it were, into his own soul.

The dream that would invite the supplicant to the sanctuary of Asklepius can be compared to an initial dream at the beginning of analytical treatment. Psychotherapists who use dream analysis in their work are often struck by the prognostic character of the initial dreams a patient brings. Some of them seem to embody both a diagnosis of the problem and a prognosis for its cure.

A deeply troubled young woman, who was greatly threatened by the unconscious and in danger of being overwhelmed and losing her bearings, had an initial dream in which a fiery red ball came whirling at her. A voice said to her that it would now be safe for her to eat the ball as I was with her. At this she took off a tiny piece of the fiery red ball and ate it. The dream shows her danger—of burning up from the heat of the energies within her—but it suggests that it will be possible for her to integrate a little bit of the unconscious at a time, with the helpful presence of another human being who understands what she is experiencing. Such a dream can be understood as an "invitation" from the unconscious for her to enter the shrine of her soul in search of healing.

Inspired to hope by his initial dreams, the patient would make a journey to a temple of Asklepius. These temples were usually out in the countryside, and often at a considerable distance, so this journey is the equivalent of the pilgrimage of which we spoke earlier. It is a sacred journey in search of healing, a journey undertaken for a holy purpose. No one becomes whole without undertaking such a journey.

It may not necessarily involve a physical journey from one place to another, but it must involve a spiritual journey in which we move from our location or attitude in the beginning to an entirely new psychological place. But often the pilgrimage in search of healing, which alone can lead to wholeness, must involve physical effort as well.

One man of my acquaintance tells of traveling three thousand miles across the United States to find the right person for him to work with in his search for healing. His long journey was preceded by many false starts as he tried first this and then that in his efforts to overcome a state of profound anxiety and depression. Without really knowing why he was doing it, he found himself making a long journey to a faraway city where, seemingly by accident, he was led to the particular person who was to influence his life so greatly. It is an example of being guided by the inner dog, something operating in the unconscious that knew what the man did not know consciously about where to find healing. It is also an example of the kind of inner and outer journey that enters into the healing process.

The healing miracles of Jesus are revealing on this point. In Greek there are several words that mean a "cure" or "healing" in the sense that a specific malady or illness is alleviated, but there is also one Greek word that means "to be saved" or "made whole" which refers to a much more inclusive healing of the total person. In the Gospels, when Jesus heals someone vicariously or at a distance, one of the lesser Greek words is used. So, for instance, when he heals the Centurion's servant the servant is "cured." Jesus in this case was acting upon the faith and insistence of the Centurion while the ailing servant stayed at home. But when someone went to Jesus personally, that is, undertook a personal pilgrimage, and was healed, Jesus used the greater Greek word and said, "Your faith has made you whole." An example is the healing of the woman with the issue of blood (Mark 5:25-34 KJV), who fought her way through a crowd of people to touch the hem of Jesus' garment. Jesus, sensing power had gone out of him, asked, "Who touched my clothes?" When the woman came forward and told him the whole truth, Jesus said, "Daughter, thy faith hath made thee whole; go in peace, and be whole of thy plague." Here is a case in which someone made a pilgrimage, inspired from within by faith, and, as a result, was made whole.

The supplicant at the shrine of Asklepius not only possessed faith, but was exercising it in a positive direction. Faith grows with use, and atrophies with disuse.

True faith is not to be confused with dogmas, creeds, or matters of intellectual belief; rather it is an emotional response, an instinctual act. To have faith is to be moved within by a powerful force, to be "gripped" by something. There is no conflict between faith, in this sense of the word, and the mind or intellect. Faith has nothing to do with blindly believing in things that cannot be intellectually demonstrated. It is not a *sacrificium intellectus*, but a motion of the soul that moves us in the direction of greater life. This faith is an all-important ingredient in healing, for without it the pilgrimage will not take place, and without faith on the part of doctor and patient alike, the healing will not occur. It is this alone that often keeps the healing process going amid the myriad times of doubt, despair, and pain. This is why it is important to act upon the faith we have even though we are assailed by doubts; in this way faith will grow.

But there must be some place to put our faith if it is to be effective. In the New Testament, the Greek work for faith means literally "to put trust into." So there must be a proper receptacle in which faith can be put. Here the temple of Asklepius was helpful, for faith could be placed in the god. In our culture, faith probably has to be placed in a special person who we feel has a skill or knowledge that can put us in touch with healing.

Once the individual arrived at the temple, we saw that he had to undergo rites of confession and purification. Until one is right with oneself and one's neighbors, the healing powers of the soul cannot be put into effect. It was at the moment of arrival that the priests at the temple required the supplicant to make amends for his sins before entering the inner sanctum to petition the god for healing. In the language of depth psychology, we call this dealing with the shadow, the inferior, unwanted part of our life and personality. Until one is willing to face one's shadow, the dark side of one's life, the unconscious simply does not open up, and the forces of healing are locked within.

Of course the supplicant knew that a confession and purification would be required of him, and we can imagine that on his journey to the temple he was engaged in taking what Alcoholics Anonymous calls his "personal inventory." He knew that he would be expected to make his life right, to set his house in order, and while this is a painful task, he was driven to it by the greater pain of his illness. This is also part of the reason wholeness is not possible without pain, for there is great resistance to seeing our shadow; few face their darkness without being driven to it by a greater pain. Yet without this self-examination, little or nothing happens.

Jung tells the story of a man who came to him after having had some previous Freudian analysis. He announced that he had gone quite carefully over his whole childhood and could rationally explain all the reasons why he was so neurotic, but in spite of his complete and expert psychological analysis he was no better. Jung says he was as puzzled as his client that there was no improvement, but finally began to inquire about his way of life. Adroit questioning revealed that the young man had no job, was not seeking work, and was living off of a hard-working woman school teacher. The woman was so lonely and had such needs that she tolerated the situation in which she supported this young man, and he was taking advantage of her need in order to indulge his laziness and hedonism. Jung confronted him with this, and assured him that until he began to carry his own share of life he could not expect improvement. This was not what the young man wanted to hear and Jung says that he saw no more of him.

A man once consulted me for relief of anxiety, insomnia, poor physical health, and drinking. I worked hard with this man for several weeks and used all the skills I could muster, but nothing seemed to improve and he eventually drifted away. Only later did I learn that he was involved in shady undertakings that eventually were exposed. He hadn't shared this dark part of his life with me, evidently hoping he could get well without having to deal with it. However, this is not possible, for healing cannot take place if we have anything to hide from ourselves or others. Our soul must be in order before God will come. The priests of Asklepius understood this, which is the reason their purificatory rites were so important.

At the temple of Asklepius, after the supplicant had satisfactorily completed his confession and purification and had prepared himself with the proper prayers, he was then ushered into the abaton. As mentioned previously, the abaton was a place not to be entered into uninvited, suggesting that if he were not invited, and still entered, he would be unwelcome and perhaps even in danger. There are dangers in contacting the powers of the unconscious without proper preparation and the proper motives. This is at least part of the reason for the unfortunate end to many drug trips, for use of a drug can plunge a person into the fireball world of the unconscious in a destructive way. The numinous energies of the inner world must be approached carefully, in the right spirit, and in a humble manner. The danger of hybris (arrogance) is always great, and may be fatal to the ego. Like Icarus, who tried to fly near the sun and was destroyed, so the arrogant ego who is not invited may be destroyed.

Once within the abaton, the supplicant was alone. We have seen that in this solitary chamber he lay on the kline, from which our modern word clinic has been derived. The entire procedure was designed to achieve a profound introversion so that a lowering of the threshold of consciousness would result. It is as though the ego has a wall around it which has the effect and function of excluding the contents of the unconscious. This is necessary, for unless the ego is protected by its wall it is in danger of being overwhelmed and can scarcely function. In cases where the wall is lacking, or has been destroyed by drugs, the doctor or therapist must work desperately with the patient to try to reconstruct the natural barriers of the ego against being inundated from within. On the other hand, unless contents from the unconscious succeed from time to time in crossing over into consciousness, the life of consciousness becomes sterile and dry and illness results. Especially in times of need and crisis a means must be found to lower the barrier between the ego and the unconscious and allow the healing powers of the inner world to enter. The psychotherapeutic systems, which have from ancient times been enshrined in the religions of the world, all have a means of doing this by excluding outer stimuli and, through solitude, making it easier for the unconscious to enter consciousness.

Today we have little respect for such introverted states; indeed we fear them, because of the general fear of the unconscious. Even if someone desires to achieve a state of incubation, a "sleeping-in" state, it is not always easy to attain, for our inner quiet is constantly disrupted by the phone, the doorbell, the television, and myriad distractions that make up modern life. The result is that the unconscious is not readily accessible to many people, for consciousness is so inundated by external distractions that the images of the inner world remain invisible. This only intensifies the problem, of course, for it amounts to a rejection of the unconscious, and often brings about dangerous manifestations of the inner world. A little goes a long way, however, and many people benefit a great deal by even one quiet evening at home, without television or radio, simply with their own thoughts, allowing the stillness to sink in. Sometimes the phone must be taken off the hook for a while to achieve this; there is no reason why our souls should have to suffer from the tyranny of modern devices and technology.

What the supplicant hoped for in the abaton was a healing dream. The dream is nature's way of allowing contents of the unconscious to come into consciousness. We will look at dreams and their meaning more closely later on, but here we can say that a dream is like the voice of our soul, and through a dream some of the unconscious enters into our conscious world. Moreover, it is a safe way. Even though a dream may be frightening, there is reason to believe

that it allows into consciousness only that which we are ready to re
ceive. To follow dreams, therefore, is not to be plunged willy-nilly
into a whirlpool of unconscious contents that might overwhelm us,
but is to allow the pleroma of the inner world to cross over into consciousness bit by bit. The whole of the inner world cannot be taken
into ourselves at once. The dream lets the inner world come in a little
at a time. So it is like a medicine that in one large dose would poison
us, but in small doses cures us. The fact that the dream was at the
center of the cult of Asklepius shows that the ancient Greeks were instinctively in touch with their inner world, as is also evidenced by the
use that the Greek physician Galen made of dreams as a means of
diagnosing and prescribing for his patients.

The journey, the purification, the consultation with the priests,
and finally the days and nights alone in the inner chamber culminat-
ing in a powerful dream, must have greatly affected the state of mind
of the supplicant. The result was an *altered state of consciousness*,
that is, a radical change and renewal of the life of the ego by means
of its contact with an irrational, energizing experience. No deep healing is possible without such an altered state of consciousness, and no
one should approach the god for healing unless he is willing to undergo it. Techniques of meditation, prayer, initiation, and incubation are
designed to produce experiences that will alter our state of consciousness, and in this way make possible the infusion of new life and
energy.

We cannot expect to remain the same if we go to a divine source
for healing. This is why those who seek to be whole must be actively
involved in the process, for without this involvement there cannot be
a change in consciousness. Today, many people want to be treated
passively. We want surgery or drugs, or we want someone to pray us
to health, or we go to one of the many sources of "packaged" healing
where someone will say to us, "Just follow these steps and pay your
money and you will find what you want." But the message from the
cult of Asklepius is that the person who wants to become whole must
be part of the great opus of healing. We must suffer our own inner
process, undergo our own journey, and have our own consciousness-
changing experience in the abaton of our souls.

There are interesting points of comparison between Asklepius
and Christ.[3] Both Christ and Asklepius were snatched from death.
Like the unborn Asklepius, the infant Christ was nearly destroyed by
Herod's soldiers, and saved only at the last moment by the divine intervention of the angel who came to his earthly father, Joseph, in a
dream and warned him to flee with the child and his mother.

Both Christ and Asklepius were healers who were mortal and immortal. Jesus of Nazareth as a human healer cast out demons and cured the sick; Asklepius, helped by the Gorgon's blood and Chiron's medical knowledge, was a successful physician who healed people wherever he went. After his death on the cross, Christ entered the realm of the dead, was resurrected and lives forever, his healing benefits being available to all mankind through his saving blood; Asklepius was killed, made his descent into Hades, was resurrected, and, as an immortal, his healing became available to all mankind.

Both Christ and Asklepius shared a divine-human birth. For Asklepius, it was the mortal mother, Coronis, and the god, Apollo. In the Christian story, it is the earthly Mary, made fertile by the power of the Holy Ghost. As we noted earlier, both Christ and Asklepius were closely associated with the feminine element, not only in their personal, charismatic gifts of sensitivity and relatedness, but also via their many women associates and friends.

Much of the symbolism is also shared in common. Like Asklepius, Christ is clearly associated with water. His baptism is a descent into water, and in the fourth chapter of John's Gospel he speaks of the living water that he has to offer mankind that will heal their thirst forever. We have noted the importance of water symbolism in Asklepian temples, and the use made of a purificatory baptism in the preparatory rites. There is also the serpent symbolism associated with Christ, which is analogous to the serpent as a symbol of the Greek god. In John 3:13-14, Jesus says of himself, "the son of Man must be lifted up as Moses lifted up the serpent in the desert, so that everyone who believes may have eternal life in him." This serpent symbolism became enshrined in the early church in the famous chalice of St. John. The legend is that the apostle John was condemned to die by drinking poison, but as he lifted the poisoned chalice to his lips, the poison was taken out of the drink in the form of a serpent. This chalice, with the serpent arising out of it, became an important symbol in the early church for the healing power of Christ.

These points of comparison were not lost upon the early Christians. At first they ascribed the similarities between Christ and Asklepius to the devil, who, they said, devised such a parallel to Christ in order to seduce Christians away from the true faith. Later, however, they did unwitting honor to the Greek god of healing by taking over the Asklepian shrines and rededicating them as places of healing under the tutelage of various Christian saints. Today, Christians do not need to be offended by the parallels between the Greek god and Christ, for underlying both are the great archetypal images and themes of healing that are common to all mankind; they have their source in the human soul regardless of the form or culture in which they appear.

This is why the cult of Asklepius and the Christian healing lore are so helpful to us today, for the archetypal themes of healing do not change. Those who are ill today can follow the path to healing laid down by the ancient Greeks, for it still lives in the human soul. True, our culture generally does not recognize the irrational nature of healing, and does not provide us with an institution dedicated to the Divine Physician. But the healing way that the cult of Asklepius provided is still in the human soul. The pilgrimage, the purification, the catharsis, the introversion, the incubation, and the healing dreams are still available to us. Contact with the soul, who knows the Way to healing, can place us once more upon the path to wholeness pioneered by the supplicants of old who sought help from the great god.

Notes

1. C.A. Meier, *Ancient Incubation and Modern Psychotherapy* (Evanston, Ill.: Northwestern University Press, 1967).

2. Doctors are referred to in Jer. 8:22, Gen. 50:2, Job 13:4, and II Chronicles 16:12. The latter reference reads: "A disease attacked Asa from head to foot in the thirty-ninth year of his reign; and, what is more, he turned in his sickness, not to Yahweh, but to doctors." The reference is somewhat derogatory because it implies that if you were truly a faithful follower of Yahweh you would not resort to doctors. The derogatory nature of the reference is reinforced by the Hebrew word, which can also be taken to mean a spirit of the underworld. Probably these physicians were pagans, and not Hebrews. There is one reference in the Apocrypha, Ecclesiasticus 38:1-14, in which doctors are mentioned in a complimentary way, but this is quite a late book.

3. There are also, of course, differences. For instance, with Christ the physical healings are manifestations of the spiritual reality of the kingdom of God. Christ is much more than a divine physician. He is also the great teacher and the one in whom a revelation of the nature of God is accomplished.

IV

The Ecstatic Healer

The cult of Asklepius told us a great deal about healing, but it did not tell us about the kind of person who is called to be a healer. The supplicant sought healing, as we saw, from the god himself; human intermediaries, such as the priests at the temples, played an important role, but were not themselves the healers. This does not tell us much about the personality of the human being who is a healer, yet in almost all times and places there has been a particular person who is looked to for healing by the people in his community.

The widespread phenomenon known as *shamanism* comes to our rescue. In Siberia, North and South America, Indonesia and Africa we find the shaman, or primitive healer, and everywhere that he exists there is a similarity in the way he is called to his vocation, how he functions, and how he understands illness. There are variations, of course, but it is possible to draw some general conclusions. The origin of the word shaman is obscure, but it seems to have come from Siberia and to be the native word for the primitive healer.

Although shamanism proper exists only in the locales already mentioned, shamanistic elements occur all over the world. The major religions of the world are all shamanistic at their core for they teach the need for a death and rebirth of the faithful, and all proclaim that in addition to the boxlike world of ego consciousness, there exists another dimension to reality. Most important, there are shamanistic personalities today. Failure to recognize them results in mismanagement of the illnesses with which these people are inevitably afflicted, and the failure of such people to find a proper spiritual life vocation.

A detailed study of shamanism, and discussion of the differences in shamanism in different regions, is beyond the scope of this book, but a general discussion of the call of the shaman, the type of person who becomes a shaman, the role of illness in creating shamans, the theory of illness with which shamans operated, and the means for curing illness will tell us a great deal about who the healer is and the mystery of healing.

The shaman could be either a man or woman. We should speak
of shamanesses as well as shamans, but for the sake of brevity and
convenience I will use the word *shaman* to mean either a man or
woman functioning as the healer. The fact that the profession of
healing was open to both sexes is noteworthy, for in all other functions in primitive society the roles of men and women were clearly
demarcated; the men had their functions and the women had theirs
and the two did not overlap. In the area of healing, however, the
usual occupational distinction between the two sexes did not prevail,
and women became shamans as often as men.

The reason for this was that a person became a shaman because
he or she was called to the vocation by the spirits. It was not a matter
of human choice, but of divine decision, and if the spirits selected a
woman to be a healer, this divine election was acknowledged by the
whole community. Since healing, as we have seen, contains an important feminine element, it is not surprising that the spirits should select
many women to function in the healing role.

The call to become a shaman was often extended to a person at
an early age, although a person did not usually function in a fully
professional way until he had reached his maturity. Black Elk, for instance, the Sioux Indian shaman whose story we will look at in more
detail shortly, was only nine years old when he received his call. A
young person who was destined to be a shaman might exhibit peculiar
behavior even before the call was extended. Unusual and vivid dreams
might come to him anticipating his divine election, or he might
wander about alone, go off in solitude for extended periods of time,
have lapses of consciousness, and display other psychic phenomena
that made him distinct from the other young people of the community. Many of these traits would, in our day, be regarded as symptoms
of mental derangement; such a young person would be regarded as
strange, and, no doubt, be encouraged to adopt more conventional
behavior. But in a primitive society, a young person exhibiting such
behavior would be looked upon differently, and the others might simply wonder if this youth was destined for a special vocation in life.

While there might be preliminary signs of a shamanic vocation,
the crucial call almost invariably came through an initiatory illness in
which the young person was exposed to the spirit world. Ancient
descriptions of such illnesses suggest a time of intense psychological
crisis, perhaps attended by physical illness or incapacitation. The candidate described his experiences in terms of dismemberment and
death; he fell grievously ill, was taken apart, lost consciousness, was
carried away by the evil spirits of illness and death. Such descriptions

suggest that the initiatory illness was experienced in a frightening and painful way, and would amount to an invasion by the unconscious, as we would say today. In time there would be a recovery from the illness, described as a feeling of being put back together, a restoration to life, and a renewal of health, but this would occur only after the candidate had heard the spirit world talking to him, had seen personally the spirits of illness and death, and had been instructed in the kind of life he was to lead. It is clear that in this preliminary illness there was extended to the young person a call to a certain kind of life, and that in his experience of approaching death, and his later restoration to life, such a person was put in touch with the underlying mysteries of illness and health. The ultimate source of his power as a healer lay in this and similar experiences. He could help others find healing because he himself had been ill and recovered and in this way had been in touch with the archetype of the Wounded Healer.

Mircea Eliade, in his fine book *Shamanism*, gives this account from a Yakut (Siberian) shaman on his type of initiatory experience. "Each shaman," the ancient Yakut records, "has a Bird-of-Prey-Mother, which is like a great bird with an iron beak, hooked claws, and a long tail. This mythical bird shows itself only twice: at the shaman's spiritual birth, and at his death. It takes his soul, carries it to the underworld, and leaves it to ripen on a branch of a pitch pine. When the soul has reached maturity the bird carries it back to earth, cuts the candidate's body into bits, and distributes them among the evil spirits of disease and death. Each spirit devours the part of the body that is his share; this gives the future shaman power to cure the corresponding diseases. After devouring the whole body the evil spirits depart. The Bird-Mother restores the bones to their place and the candidate wakes as from a deep sleep."[1]

Such a description strikes us as fanciful today only because it uses a primitive, mythological language to describe psychological states. For those who know the psyche, it is clear that it is a description of a person whose ego has been taken down to its bare bones, to the very essentials, and who has suffered a deep invasion from the unconscious. It is this immediate contact with the unconscious, which primitive people call the spirit world, which is the characteristic quality of the shamanistic personality. The bare-bones quality of such initiatory experiences was represented in the shaman's costume which frequently contained the design of a skeleton. When a shaman performed his healing function, he wore a religious garb, just as a modern priest wears certain specified vestments to celebrate the Eucharist. The skeleton on the shaman's garb symbolized that profound, all-important initiatory experience that had taken him down to his most naked self, and then restored him again to the fullness of life.

Most records of shamanistic experiences are ancient, but there are a few that are close to our time. One of the most interesting of these is told by Black Elk, a Sioux Indian shaman who lived in the latter part of the 19th and early part of the 20th centuries. Black Elk tells us the story of his initiatory illness and call in his autobiography, *Black Elk Speaks*.[2]

Black Elk first began to hear the spirits speak to him when he was a very young boy, and at first, of course, he did not understand what was happening to him. "Now and then," he relates, "the voices would come back when I was out alone, like someone calling me, but what they wanted me to do I did not know." This is typical of the kind of experience that comes to a person who is destined to be set aside for the spiritual vocation; he begins to be aware of a presence or reality others do not notice, but at first he does not understand it.

Gradually the voices became more insistent, and one day Black Elk heard a voice that said to him: "It is time; now they are calling you." He decided he should go, and started out of the tepee, but his thighs began to hurt him and by the next morning he was very ill, eventually lapsing into a state of unconsciousness that lasted for twelve days. His parents hovered over him anxiously as he lay in this deathlike state, but he tells us that all this time he was not there in his body at all. As the illness fell upon him the voices called to him: "Hurry! Come! Your Grandfathers are calling you!"

Black Elk then describes a complicated and remarkable vision. It takes him twenty-five pages to give us a summary of this experience. Eventually he was shown the center of the world, a high mountain from which he could see the "whole hoop of the world." Later he identified this mountain with Harney Peak in the Black Hills, but he also noted, "but anywhere is the center of the world" (p. 43). This tells us that he recognized his experience as an interior experience, a journey into the microcosm of his own spiritual space.

Finally Black Elk was escorted back to earth. As he entered his tepee and saw his mother and father bending over a sick boy who was himself, he heard someone saying: "The boy is coming to; you had better give him some water" (p. 47). He soon recovered from his illness and was glad to be back with his parents and people again, but was also sad because he felt everyone should know about his vision. He was afraid to tell it to them, however, as he was so young he was sure they wouldn't believe him. This had a negative effect upon him later and when he was a grown young man, he again became ill. This time he developed a neurosis, a nervous instability characterized by vaguely defined but crippling waves of anxiety.

Finally Black Elk consulted his uncle, the shaman Black Road, who advised him to perform his youthful vision for his people, and then he would be healed. So Black Elk and Black Road made plans for a gigantic village festival in which the whole Indian community would assist in acting out the mighty vision, and thus a ritual was born, for a ritual is a dramatic representation of a powerful visionary experience.

As a result of the dramatization of his vision, Black Elk was healed of his neurosis. It was not only that he had benefited by the catharsis that he had undergone when he told his uncle his experience, nor even that he regained health through a kind of psychodrama with the village people. More than that, Black Elk's experience belonged to his people, not just to him, and he would have remained sick until he had done the right thing with it.

This is characteristic of shamanistic experiences. The person called to be a shaman must learn to shamanize, that is, must take his powerful experiences and find a way to share the power with his people. If he does not shamanize, he will become ill again and may die, for the shaman is called to a certain kind of life, and if he does not lead it properly, his power will turn against him and kill him. This is why Black Elk fell ill a second time, and why he recovered, for after the dramatic representation of his vision, Black Elk went on to become a spiritual leader and healer of his people.

Black Elk's story contains the essentials of shamanistic experience: preliminary signs of being called by the spirit world, an initiatory illness, a time of instruction from the powers of the spirit world, a return to health and earthly life, and the imperative to lead a special kind of existence.

Sometimes illness comes to the shaman not once but many times, each instance being the call to a further step in consciousness. One African tribe, for instance, reports twelve stages of development, each ushered in by an illness. Not all the shamans, called in this tribe "sangomas," will go through all twelve stages, but those who do will acquire the most spiritual power. Adrian K. Boshier, explorer and anthropologist, who has lived with African people for extended periods of time, reports on the initiatory illness of a shamaness by the name of Dorcas.[3] Dorcas told him, he relates, "that no one becomes a sangoma without first getting sick. Everyone who is called by the spirits gets the sickness, a bad sickness. No one can become a sangoma who does not get this. You must tell people what happens to us, all the sangomas when that spirit calls them. Oh! How hard it is and how we must work with those spirits!"

Dorcas is herself a prime illustration of the initiatory illness of the shaman, and her story, told in her own words, is worth repeating in its entirety.

"The sangoma," she told Boshier, "is a person with a strong spirit. All people have a spirit, black people, white people, Chinese people, but God chooses some to talk through. It is like he gives some people a gift. All have spirit, but for some it is a gift, and those people become sangomas. Like Jesus, do you know Jesus? God gave him a big, big gift, a large spirit. Many of the people didn't understand this about him. But he had that spirit. He walked alone in the mountains, didn't he? He talked with his spirits, didn't he? He made sick people better, didn't he? It is just like that. But you must go out—you must go out into the mountains, you know. How can you know anything if you don't go out? How can people learn about the spirits of the mountains and the rivers if they just go to the university? No, to learn about the spirits you must go out alone into the wild places.

"When my spirit came I was sick—Oh! I was so sick! I lay in bed for three years—I could not eat or drink or even walk. I just lay there day after day and at night dreams would come! At night I would leave my body and my spirit would go far, far away to other places that my body never sees. My spirit would see so many things in the night. And then in the morning, before the sun comes up, my spirit would return to my body, and I would lay in bed another day.

"I went to many white doctors and black medical doctors. I was a Christian—my father was a Methodist minister—and I wanted the medical doctors to make me better. None of them could find what was wrong with me, none of them could cure me. Finally, at Baragwanath Hospital a Dr. Steyn told me, 'You must go to your own doctors. They can help you and we cannot.' He knew. But still I would not go.

"One night, in a dream, my grandfather came to see me and told me, 'You are not sick. You are going to help your people. I like you very much, and my spirit will enter your body, and you will do my work.' But I still wanted nothing to do with it. I was a Christian and I wanted nothing of that sangoma business.

"The sangomas would visit me and tell me that I had the spirit. But I told my mother to send them away. I did not want to hear them! At night the sangomas would come in my dreams and shout at me that I must become sangoma. I did not want to hear it. I asked my mother to move my bed into the other room. But they even found me there in the lounge. My mother got so tired taking care of me, she finally told me, 'Oh, Dorcas, I wish God would take you now.' But he did not take me and those spirits did not leave me alone. They came so strong it was like at the cinema, the pictures came before my eyes just like they were real. My eyes saw everything, but my body could not move. They came all the time to me, shouting and showing me things like beads, skins and herbs. But still I would not give in. 'I am a Christian, not a sangoma! You must go away.' But they would not go away.

"One night they came in my dreams, while I was sleeping in the lounge. There were many of them and they sat at the foot of my bed on that long bench there. They were just like real people. Big, big sangomas they were. They sat there and they ordered me to sing. They clapped their hands and they sang a song which I can still remember. They said, 'Sing!' There was one very big fat sangoma. She told me, 'Get up! Get up and sing! You are sangoma, you are not sick! Wake up—you must wake up and teach!' Then they just disappeared.

"One night in a dream they showed me a headdress I must make out of beads and wool. I did make that headdress, with the long wool strands like sangoma hair, and beads on all the strands. I did not wear it, but I did make it. Finally, one night my grandfather came to me in a dream and told me, 'You must wear it. If you do not wear it I will kill you!'

"At this point I went to the Apostolic Church who said they would cure me. They carried me to a river, and put me in that water right up to my neck. But then, when I was in that river, I suddenly felt something under my feet. It lifted me right up. I was terrified! I leapt out of that river and saw that it was a big snake—it was my grandfather! At that point the Apostolic Church gave up. They said, 'Your grandfather wants you to become sangoma, and we can do nothing. You must give in.' At home that night I talked with my father and he said to me that even though he was a Methodist minister he knew that my spirit was that of a sangoma.

"The next day my mother took me to my auntie's house, my auntie who is sangoma. At her house all the sangomas came to see me. They beat the drum and said, 'Get up and dance!' I did get up. I did dance and I did sing. Hours and hours it was like to me, singing and dancing. For three years I had not been able to walk. Now, this day, I was dancing! The sangomas all laughed and laughed at me, and I could not stop dancing. Finally I fell back to bed, exhausted. My training had begun. That was in 1962. Oh! What a time that was, when I started to dance and gave in to the spirits!"[4]

Dorcas's story is typically shamanistic. She was called to become a healer, and experienced the call through an acute crisis, remaining ill until she agreed to live the life of a sangoma. There is an implication in her story that if she had heeded the call when it first came, it might not have been necessary for her to be ill, but in point of fact she was ill for three long years before she accepted what was required of her.

It might be, as my friend and colleague Robert Johnson once suggested to me, that if we understood our destiny properly at the beginning, and carried its suffering correctly, we would not need to become ill. Something like this evidently happened with Dr. Jung. His direct encounter with the unconscious, which he describes for us in chapter six of his autobiography, *Memories, Dreams, Reflections,* was a shamanistic type of experience. There is no indication, however, that he became ill at this time, evidently because he was able to understand enough of what his experience meant. Had this understanding and development not taken place, he would certainly have become ill. However, in the overwhelming majority of cases such understanding is not possible; the experience is resisted or misunderstood, and illness follows. In any event, the result of the encounter with the spirit world is a drastic and forcible change of personality, justifiably likened to a death and rebirth experience. The great suffering this brings must be properly carried if the intended new consciousness is to come about.

The stories of Black Elk and Dorcas, and shamanistic tradition in general, tell us that illness can be a form of initiation. Paradoxically, as was suggested in chapter two, to become whole certain people may first have to become ill. Looked at in this light we cannot say that a person who never suffers evidence of malfunctioning is whole; such a person may simply have never been touched by the powers within, and so may never reach his maximum possible development. For illness can have the affect of dissolving (dismembering) our conscious personality in such a way that an entirely new state of consciousness is allowed to emerge.

The alchemists called this state the *solutio*. Everything is dissolved, but in this state of dissolution, which is certainly experienced in a painful way, a new personality develops, a personality formed from within, from the deepest inner Center. The end result of such an illness is a *creative cure*, that is, the individual recovers from his illness in such a way that he becomes a far more conscious and developed person than he was before.

This is quite a different theory of illness than that commonly held today, in which no inner meaning is attached to our painful state, and efforts at healing are simply directed toward a restoration of the previous level of functioning. When this is the only healing that can be effected, the net result is a diminution of personality. We can never simply return to the condition in which we were before our crisis, without the scope of our personality being reduced. If we do so it amounts to what Jung called "the regressive restoration of the persona." This truth applies to everyone, whether we are called upon to function as a healer or not, for there is something of the shaman in each person, and there is something shamanistic about every illness. Unless the meaning of our illness is made conscious, our healing will not be complete and its intended goal will not be renewed. Moreover, in all of us, the price of continued health is the continued development of consciousness. The ever-present threat of regression stands at our backs like a monster, and impels us forward on the journey toward an ever-expanding conscious development. To refuse the journey is to run the risk of incurring the fate of Lot's wife (Gen. 19:26).

We are now in a position to see the difference between the shaman and the priest as he functions today. As Sheldon Kopp pointed out in a searching article, the priest in our times is the exponent of a collective, institutionalized religion; he functions on behalf of a tradition, and represents an embodied doctrine and collective religious attitude.[5] The generic aspect of the priest is represented in Christendom by the tendency of certain churches to call their priests by the title of Father. This means that the priest's individual humanity is subordinated to his collective functioning as a personification of the father spirit of his particular religious denomination. Behind the priest is a hallowed religious institution that empowers the priest to act in the name of God and gives him his authority. The soul of the individual is not to be listened to for its own sake, but is to be fitted into the existing system.

If we go back far enough into the history of the religious institution the priest represents, we will find that this institution originated from powerful, personal, spiritual experiences that came to certain individuals, but these individual experiences have long since become codified and solidified into a religious structure. In the Old Testament we have the original experiences of the prophets in which men like Moses, Isaiah, and Ezekiel were spoken to directly by God. Later these personal experiences were institutionalized into the Judaic religion. In Christianity we have the unique relationship between Jesus and his Heavenly Father, and the immediate religious experiences of the apostles. However, within a few centuries these personal experiences became enshrined in the Christian Church with its tradition, ritual, and doctrine. In this way an original, primary religious experience of certain individuals became the secondary religious experience of the masses. Thus most people do not *know* God, but only hear about Him through the experiences of others, and religious structures that claim to lead people to God may, in fact, serve to keep people from God by shielding them from their own experience with the numinous.

The shaman, on the other hand, derives his power from a personal, direct encounter with the numinous inner world; he has his own encounter with the unconscious. The effectiveness of a shaman in helping others stems from the shaman's own depth of experience. The shaman is an individual, and can only help people in an individual way by helping them relate to their personal, inner experiences, not to an institutionalized faith.

Shamanism flourished particularly among primitive people whose way of life was founded primarily upon hunting, perhaps because hunting societies stressed the importance of the individual hunter and his achievements. Shamanistic cultures recognized the special call of certain people to function as healers, as we have seen, but also recognized that each individual in the community had a certain calling from the spirit world and could be given a certain power. The difference between a shaman and his fellows was one of degree and of calling. Every American Indian, for instance, sought religious power —mana or "medicine"—which came through a direct relationship with the spirit world, and any Indian in a shamanistic culture who fell ill sought an individual healing experience. This is in marked contrast to our methods of healing today, in which healing is collectivized, and virtually no effort is made to discover its meaning for the individual. As a result, many people remain ill, or have to settle for a mediocre mode of functioning in life. It would seem, as Sheldon Kopp wrote, that it is time once again to have shamans as well as priests in our midst.

After the call was recognized and accepted, the young candidate began his training. Typically, this involved a long apprenticeship with an older, recognized shaman. From him he learned the techniques of his profession, both natural, medical knowledge, and spiritual techniques. The natural, medical knowledge included a knowledge of herbs and their curative powers, and methods of treating ills and injuries through physical means. Some shamans might also become skilled in rudimentary surgery, and learn how to set bones and bind up wounds. Primitive medicine among the American Indians, for instance, was fairly effective when it came to treating injuries or illnesses in which the nature of the problem was obvious. Indian doctors were as good as their European counterparts when it came to treating fractures and wounds, and even practiced trephination with considerable skill. Perhaps they were better, for they were free of certain European medical errors, such as the practice of bleeding. George Washington might have survived his final illness had he been treated by an Indian doctor, for his European-trained physician bled the feverish Washington three times in one day, which certainly must have weakened him greatly. Some Indian doctors specialized in herbology or surgery, for shamans had their specialties just as do modern doctors.

But the primary function of the shaman was in spiritual medicine, which was required whenever the cause of the illness was not obvious, as in the case of an infectious illness, or when a patient did not recover as he should from a wound or external injury. Training for the spiritual side of his profession required the shaman to become an expert in the mythological lore of his tribe, and in the art of drumming and chanting, for it was in this way that the spirits were summoned to his aid or the shaman would transport himself out of his body and into the spirit world. In some ancient societies there was a secret language known only to the shamans; by means of this the shamans said they could talk to the animals and the birds, and commune with the spirit world.

The period of apprenticeship lasted a long time, the training always being one-to-one, not in a school. The candidate would choose his mentor, and if the older shaman agreed, the two formed their own relationship. Of course the older shaman would be paid for his service, either directly with property or through services rendered for him by his student.

But even though the shaman-to-be had professional training from his earthly tutor, his primary education continued to be from the spirit world, for the shaman continued to learn from the spirits by means of direct communication with them. This instruction from the spirits might be carried on through dreams, for the shaman was a person to whom the spirits spoke frequently and vividly in dreams and visions. Quite often the shaman acquired a tutelary spirit, a particular spiritual being who became his instructor, who would come to the young shaman and guide him in the things he was to know. With male shamans this tutelary spirit was feminine and was regarded as his celestial wife. The shaman had two wives: his earthly wife, and his heavenly wife, and proper attention had to be given to each. In shamanesses, the tutelary spirit was always masculine, and was like her celestial husband. If she were married, she would have to give allegiance to both her earthly husband and her heavenly husband. This makes sense when we remember that the unconscious of a man is partly feminine, and is often personified as a female figure, while the unconscious of a woman carries a corresponding masculine personification.

The continuing relationship between the shaman and the spiritual world, and the ongoing instruction the shaman received from his inner partners, testifies to the recognition on the part of primitive people that healing is a charismatic function, and that the healer gains his or her efficacy from personal experience with the spirit world, resulting in the accumulation of mana or spiritual potency. The professional training was a helpful adjunct, but the power to heal could not be transmitted by human means; it could only be given directly by the spirits. This is in direct contrast to our own day when we suppose that persons in the healing professions can acquire what they need to know in schools. A certain amount of technical knowledge, perhaps, can be acquired in this way, but knowledge of the unconscious and those personal qualities that alone can give a person the capacity to deal with things of the soul cannot be transmitted in this manner. They come today, as in ancient times, from the development of personality, and a direct contact between an individual and his own soul.

The primary skill the shaman must learn is the capacity for *ecstasy*. The word ecstasy means literally to be out of oneself. Whenever our center of consciousness has shifted out of our usual here-now ego framework, and we stand apart from ourselves in a different frame of reference, we are in a state of ecstasy. It was an experience of ecstasy that came to the young candidate in his initiatory vision and illness. Black Elk, for instance, experienced a state of being out of himself in his great vision. The shaman had to acquire the capacity to go out of himself at will. To do this he had to master the art of trance, or become skilled in dream-travel. In other words, he learned how to enter into an altered state of consciousness for the purpose of summoning the spirits to the aid of his patients, or for the purpose of going in search of his patient's soul, for reasons we will look at in a moment. What first happened to him involuntarily, he later had to acquire as a technique that could be consciously directed.

The Bible abounds in examples of ecstasy. Some that come to mind are Moses on Mt. Sinai, Jesus on the Mount of Transfiguration, and Ezekiel when he was caught up by the Spirit. The most unusual example, however, occurs in the second chapter of the Book of Daniel in which we find the extraordinary story of how Daniel learned of King Nebuchadnezzar's dream. The King had dreamt, but could not recall his dream. He knew it was important, however, and called together his magicians and dream-interpreters and demanded that they interpret his dream for him. They declared they would be happy to do this if the King would only tell them what the dream was. This seems like a reasonable position to take, but Nebuchadnezzar was not a reasonable man and declared that unless they could tell him his dream and its meaning, he would execute all the dream-interpreters in the land. Now this also included Daniel and his three friends. When Daniel got word of the impending doom, he called his three friends together and got them to pray that he would receive the King's dream while he went into a trance. In Daniel's trance, he was told by God what Nebuchadnezzar's dream was, and was able to interpret it successfully, thus saving the heads of the magicians of the land.

Biblical scholars are skeptical of the historicity of most of the Book of Daniel, but this story is typically shamanic, and illustrates the shamanistic capacity to enter into special states of consciousness. Modern knowledge of depth psychology lends considerable credibility to the possibility of entering special states of consciousness, and makes it believable that someone could, as Daniel did, contact the unconscious psyche of someone else. Records of unusual powers gained in altered states of consciousness keep recurring in the annals of psychology and shamanic lore. The ancient shamans, for instance, were regarded as masters over heat and fire. They felt intense heat in their bodies while in their unusual states, and many cases are reported in which the shamans were immune to burning from fire. This reminds us that contemporary spiritual healers, during their states of spiritual concentration and prayer, experience unusual heat emanating from their bodies, or an energy that flows through their hands and into their patients.

The shaman's capacity for ecstasy makes him a master of the mystical geography of the spiritual world—the unconscious. He has an intimate and personal knowledge of these mysterious regions of the spirit, which he can enter into and return from at will. From this he derives his capacity to go to the aid of his patient whose soul, as we shall see, may have wandered into the spirit regions.

Everywhere we find shamanistic cultures, we find that the geography of the spiritual world is in three layers: there is the earth plane, the celestial world above, and the world below or the underworld. This three-tier spiritual universe is joined at the center of the world. If one can find this center of the world, one has the capacity to move at will from one layer of reality to another. At this Cosmic Center is the World Tree, and if one climbs to the top of this mighty tree, one finds oneself in the world above. There is also the Cosmic Mountain of which Black Elk spoke, whose heights reached up to the celestial region. Or there is the Celestial Rope or Ladder which can be climbed up or down, giving access to worlds above, such as Jacob's ladder which he saw in his famous dream, on which angels were ascending and descending from heaven to earth and back again. The shaman is the person who has been taken to this Cosmic Center and knows how to find it again, and so has the power to move from one level of reality to another.

The earth layer can be taken as a symbol for the ego and its frame of reference. This is ordinary reality, life as we experience it in our customary waking state, a here-now reality. The celestial world and the underworld symbolize different modes of reality or different psychic states in which a person has moved away from the ego and is experiencing the unconscious. There is no moral difference between the worlds above and below. The underworld is not a place of evil; the spirits who dwell there are just different from the spirits of the upper world, generally being more chthonic and darker in nature. Shamans usually moved from the earth plane to the world above or to the world below, but seldom to both realms, so, according to his needs, a person who wanted a shaman's help would seek out either the "White Shaman," who had access to heaven, or the "Black Shaman," who had access to the world below.

The story of Jack and the Beanstalk comes to mind. In this ancient tale the hero, Jack, lives with his mother in a little cabin in the woods. They are very poor and eventually have only one miserable cow left to them, which Jack's mother tells him to sell in the market. On the way Jack meets a strange old man with a long white beard who inquires where Jack is going with his cow. "To the market to sell her," Jack replies. "No need to go that far," the old man says, "for I will give you these three bright colored beans for her." Jack is so captivated by the beans that he exchanges the cow for them and runs home with them to his mother. Of course she is furious when she finds the poor bargain he has struck; the beans are hurled out the window, and Jack is sent to bed.

In the middle of the night Jack wakens and in the moonlight sees that a gigantic beanstalk has risen from the place where the beans fell on the ground. Curious, Jack climbs to the top of the beanstalk, high, high up in the sky and here finds a gigantic castle in which lives a ferocious giant who eats small boys. Undaunted, Jack steals from the giant, first his purse of money and later, on a return journey, his magical goose that lays a golden egg upon command. Jack also succeeds in killing the giant. The enraged giant pursues Jack down the beanstalk but Jack reaches the ground first, chops the beanstalk down and the giant is killed in the fall. From then on Jack and his mother have all they need, for whenever they are in want, Jack simply says to the goose, "Lay!" and the goose lays another golden egg.

Here we see elements of the shamanic cosmology. There is an upper realm that contains great treasure, but is also dangerous, and there is a magical beanstalk that provides a means of ascent to this celestial region and a way to return again. The fairy tale is particularly reminiscent of childhood when every boy or girl has a magical connection to the rich world of fantasy from which come the treasures of the soul, but it is a dangerous world, for if one gets caught in it, one can be eaten and cannot escape, that is, cannot return to ordinary reality. The chopping down of the beanstalk suggests the severing of the connection between the ego and the fantasy world of childhood, and even though Jack winds up with the goose that lays the golden eggs, there is a feeling of disappointment that some remnant of connection between the two worlds was not kept, for the tragedy of adult life frequently lies in exactly this loss of connection with the world of the unconscious and its imagery, which was so close to us as children.

The capacity of the shaman to move from ordinary reality to mystical reality was essential in terms of the primitive theory of illness. Illness came from two primary causes, except, as mentioned before, when there was an obvious external injury or wound. First, it might be caused by the presence within a person of a magical foreign object, and if so it was the task of the shaman to discover this object and remove it. You might, for instance, be journeying through the forest and be struck by a fairy dart shot at you by an unseen malignant spirit who, perhaps, had been sent by an enemy to wound you. The shaman would call upon his helping spirits, or use his dreams, to diagnose the cause of the unknown illness, and if the illness was diagnosed as caused by such a foreign object, it would be removed with great ceremony, usually by suction. Sometimes a small stone or other object would be cast away by the shaman as convincing proof to others who were watching that the cause of the illness had been discovered and banished.

But the illness might be caused by the separation of the person's soul from his body. As long as body and soul were conjoined and in the proper relationship, a person would be healthy, but if the soul and body became separated, illness would result, and if the separation became permanent, death would be inevitable. Today we think of the body as generating that psychic life we call personality, and if someone's body perishes, we think the personality dies with it. But primitive people reversed this. To them, a body lived because a soul had come into it; the body was quickened to life by the spirit. To them this seemed obvious, because just before death a person's breath left, and to them this departing breath was the spirit or soul leaving its physical home. The inertness of the physical body after the last breath had left was an obvious proof that it was the spirit or soul that had quickened a body to life.

There were several ways the soul could become separated from the body. For instance, a person's soul might wander away and not be able to find its way back. This might happen in sleep, for in some primitive cultures it was believed that dreams came when the soul left the body and went on a journey through the spiritual world. For this reason, it was dangerous to waken someone suddenly lest his soul not have a chance to return to his body in time. In other cases, an evil demon may have taken the soul and abducted it or seduced it away. In cases of a mortal illness, the soul might be on its way to the land of departed spirits.

In any case, the shaman had the task of finding his patient's soul and rejoining it with his body. To do this, the shaman might have to leave his own body and travel in search of his patient's soul in the spiritual regions, hence the importance of the shaman's capacity for ecstasy. The shaman was aided in his diagnosis and spiritual journey by his helping spirits, and was able to find his patient's soul and return with it because of his knowledge of mystical geography, a knowledge that, as we have seen, came to him through his own personal experiences. He might also have to fight with demonic powers, or find some way of tricking them into releasing his patient's soul if the soul had been spirited away. If the soul was speeding on its way to the land of departed spirits, the shaman could pursue it and try to persuade it to return, but if the soul had gone too far, the shaman could do nothing, for the soul was now close to the land of the departed, and when this was reached the earthly person would die.

The shaman's profession was a dangerous one, for in spite of his knowledge and skill he might become lost on his ecstatic journeys, or lose the battle with the demons, in which case his own soul might be forfeited. Shamans were also sometimes accused by other members of their community of instigating illness or otherwise using their powers for evil purposes, and, of course, if they failed in their efforts to cure the sick they might be rejected and even killed.

That shamans took their task of healing seriously is evidenced in the famous death march of the Cherokee nation known as the "Trail of Tears." In 1839, the Cherokees, then living in the southeastern part of the United States, were compelled by the United States government, in spite of previous treaties, to give up their lands and move to reservations west of the Mississippi. Promised provisions for their journey were not delivered and on the long, sad march from their homes the Cherokees suffered terribly from spiritual deprivation, hunger, and exposure to the cold winter weather. A scourge of disease swept through the weakened Indians and it is estimated that four thousand of them, one-fifth of the entire nation, perished from pneumonia, tuberculosis, pellagra, and, of course, the inevitable smallpox. It is said that many of their shamans, in anguish because they could not cure their people of these diseases, most of which came from the white man, committed suicide.

Though there were shamans who used their powers for evil purposes, and could be hired by someone to send illness into an enemy by means of magic, most shamans were not only healers of the sick, but defenders of the community against evil. "In a general way," Eliade writes in his fine book on shamanism mentioned earlier, "it can be said that shamanism defends life, health, fertility, the world of 'light,' against death, diseases, sterility, disaster, and the world of 'darkness.' " So shamans were called upon for help during diverse times of spiritual adversity. At the time of death, for instance, the shamans might be asked to speed the soul of the departed on its way to the land of departed spirits. This both aided the soul of the departed to reach its proper resting place, and protected the living from the ever-present danger of possession by the ghost of the deceased. This was always a possibility until the dead person's soul was safely on its way to its new home, for the dead were lonely at first and until they knew where to go, they might seek to rejoin the living.

Shamans were also diviners, a skill that was especially required in times of war or national crisis. The Navajos, for instance, when they were still a free people in the 19th century, knew of a place in their sacred river which they called the "Shining Sands of Prophecy." Here the current of the river made ever-shifting patterns in the fine sands, and the trained eyes of the shamans of the tribe would read the meaning of the times for the Navajo people from the shifting shapes made in the sand. The wisdom of the shifting sands was consulted only in times of national emergency, and the whole people, as well as the shamans who undertook the pilgrimage to the river, had to implore divine help if the symbolic design the gods had written in the sand was to be correctly understood. Apparently such a pilgrimage by the Navajo shamans was undertaken as recently as 1929.[6]

A study of shamanism gives us information about the personality of the healer that we did not find in the healing cult of Asklepius, but the same thing that was true of Asklepius is also true of the shaman: they are Wounded Healers. As we saw, the invitation to the shamanic vocation comes through an illness or severe psychological crisis that is likened to death. This is followed by a rebirth, but as a result of the violent struggle to regain health, the personality of the shaman is greatly enlarged. He becomes a more conscious person because of his woundedness, and is henceforth the one in the community who, because of his experience, has direct intercourse and communication with the world of spirits. From this personal encounter with the spirit world, the shaman gains his power to heal, but the condition that must be met if he is to retain his health is that he serve the spirit world and his fellows in a lifelong work of healing.

Shamanistic elements can be seen, not only in primitive cultures, but in many famous people and world religions. Joan of Arc, for instance, was a type of shaman. She, too, heard the spirits and had to do their bidding or fall ill. The Old Testament prophets were shamanic in character except that their spiritual energy was directed to social and political concerns rather than to healing. Jesus was distinctly shamanistic. He, too, talked with his spirits, as is exemplified in the story of the Temptations in the Wilderness and the frequent sojourns he spent alone in communion with God. Like the shamans, Jesus healed the sick and was on familiar terms with the denizens of the spiritual world. Luke wrote of him, for instance, "In the synagogue there was a man who was possessed by the spirit of an unclean devil, and it shouted at the top of its voice, 'Ha! What do you want with us, Jesus of Nazareth? Have you come to destroy us? I know who you are: the Holy One of God.' " (Luke 4:33-34) And, of course, Jesus' death on the cross, his descent into the underworld, and his final ascent to heaven, were shamanistic in character, and are reminiscent of the shamans' three-layer universe.

But perhaps most important of all is the fact that many people today have a shamanistic type of calling. Certain people who fall ill in our time, as well as in times past, are being called to a special life of consciousness and spiritual development, and may even be summoned via their illness to function as healers. In such cases their illness is not healed unless its meaning can be discovered, that is, unless a *creative cure* can be found. Indeed, each person in whom individuation occurs, that is, who begins to develop into a whole person, has something of the shamanistic experience. Illness is an inevitable part of the lives of such people, and their growth takes place via a process of death and rebirth that forces them to find their own unique personality and special way of life.

In our day, we speak of the unconscious rather than of the spirit world, but it is the same reality that lies behind both shamanism and contemporary healing of the psyche. To have a direct experience with the unconscious is to begin to step into a shamanistic type of consciousness. Just as the shaman possessed a firsthand knowledge of his celestial world, so today some people are called upon to explore the geography of the inner world of the unconscious.

Today's healer, insofar as that person has spiritual and psychological qualifications as well as technical ones, will find much in the shamanic tradition that will throw light upon his development and function. Like the shamans, persons who are meant to work in the healing field are Wounded Healers. If a person has gone through a crisis, died to an old personality, and fought his or her way back to health and a more conscious life, that person may gain a certain quality that enables him to put others in touch with healing too. A certain faith in the healing process is generated by having found healing oneself, not to mention a capacity for empathy with those who are ill, which can only come through having suffered.

Most important, the modern healer, like the ancient shaman, gains a certain kind of inner quality through direct contact with the unconscious. It is not a quality to be used for egocentric or personal power purposes; if that takes place, destructive things happen. At this point true religion becomes magic, magic being defined as the use of one's knowledge of divine forces for the purposes of the ego, or to manipulate life. When someone attempts to manipulate people or destiny by means of spiritual knowledge, this is magic and it brings extreme spiritual danger with it. But used properly, the inner power of the healer is effective, even crucial, in the healing process, not so much by the direct application of his spiritual knowledge, as by the interaction that takes place between the personality of the healer and the patient.

The shaman, as we saw, went in search of his patient's lost soul. Few people today are masters of the trance state that often characterized shamanistic healing, but the psychotherapist does in certain ways function as such a soul-person by virtue of his capacity to detach his interest and concentration from himself and devote it to his client as he follows his client's story, takes part in his emotions, and is with him in his sufferings, searchings, and dreams. This "going with another person" is an ecstatic journey in the sense that the therapist steps into another person's life and psyche. He does this, not in the interest of converting the other person to anything, but in order to help the other person find his or her own unique way. It would be too much to say that the psychotherapist finds another person's soul, though often the soul hangs in balance between the therapist and the client, forming that unusual relationship known as the "transference." But often this entering of the therapist in the client's life proves crucial in the discovery by the client of what his own soul is, so that the therapist's capacity to travel through the world of someone else's emotions and dreams may prove vital to a cure.

It is not unusual in the practice of psychotherapy to have a person come in for only a few appointments and then leave feeling much better. Often a person will say, "I don't know why I feel better but I do." The improvement often comes about without any deep understanding of the problem or change in the outer situation. But, in addition to the healing forces constellated by the pilgrimage, and the act of faith that going to the appointments represented, there was also the meaningful understanding and help of another person. This in itself has a healing effect.

Robert Lindner, in his book *The Fifty Minute Hour*,[7] gives us an illustrative story of the healing power of such "soul-travel" on the part of the healer, and also of its dangers. A brilliant physicist had been sent to him because he had become psychotic. In his psychosis, the physicist believed himself to be engaged in extraordinary space travel, and was so identified with fantasies about spectacular voyages into outer space that he had lost contact with ordinary reality. Lindner decided to treat his patient by simply listening to his fantasies and entering into them. For many months he listened carefully as the physicist told him of voyages to outer space, and he became quite engrossed in the fascinating tales that were spun.

After quite a long time of this careful listening and participation, Lindner became aware that he himself was succumbing to the fascination of his patient's fantasies. At first he attempted to rationalize this, but he could not continue to ignore the signs of obsession and began to have times of acute psychic distress. Finally, one day when the patient came for his usual session with Dr. Lindner, he was restless and dispirited and had no enthusiasm or interest in any discussion that Lindner initiated.

After some probing questioning, the physicist told Lindner that for quite some time he had been making up the fantasies; they were no longer genuine. He had realized, after Lindner was sharing his delusion with him so completely, that his fantasies were just that, and he no longer believed in them. This meant, of course, that he was cured of his psychosis, for he was now able to distinguish between inner and outer reality. But he didn't know how to tell the doctor this. When Dr. Lindner asked, "Why did you pretend? Why did you keep on telling me . . . ?" the physicist replied, "Because I felt I had to. Because you wanted me to!"

Lindner writes that he then realized how close he himself had come to losing the distinction between inner and outer reality. He had become so absorbed in his patient's fantasy world that he had become more identified with it as his patient had become less identified. Such are the dangers of the healer's vocation! But the participation by Lindner in his patient's inner world—a good example of "soul-travel" —had effected the cure. There is only room for one person in a psychosis. As soon as two people are in, there is a cure, providing, of course, that one of them realizes the difference between inner and outer realities. If a number of people enter the fantasy system and accept it literally, we have, not psychosis in the psychiatric sense, but a cult or ism.

As we saw in this case, there are dangers in the healing profession today as in times past. To go with a person who searches for his or her soul is to expose oneself perilously to the other person's psyche. One can lose one's way in this, and become infected by another person's illness. The modern healer must protect himself against these dangers by being well grounded in himself, and by finding ways to purge himself of the psyche of others and get back into his own soul, so that he does not lose himself by a disastrous identification with his patients.

Like the shamans of old, the contemporary healer of the soul is also subject to all manner of projections. The shamans who failed to cure, we noted, were often in danger from their fellows; a lot was expected of the spiritual doctor, and his standing with the community was continually on the line. A healer today will also find himself the object of all kinds of unrealistic expectations, magical projections, and demands. These constitute a hazard for him, for if he identifies with what is projected upon him, he becomes inflated and begins to live through his patients and their fantasies about him. The whole relationship then becomes dangerously unrealistic, and the therapist is drawn away from living his own life. There is also the great drain upon his psychic energies that results from his "soul-travels" with his clients. Being emptied this psychological way, day in and day out, can lay the therapist open to his own ills, so that the healer must find ways to recharge his batteries and get back into himself if he is to maintain his health. This is also one reason the therapist gets paid. The payment of a fee represents a return of energy to the therapist in exchange for the energy he or she has put out on behalf of the client. It is also a compensation for the psychic contamination that living closely to another person's unconscious always brings.

To a large extent, the antidote to these dangers is the realization by therapist and client alike that the ultimate source of healing lies beyond human personalities, and exists, as the cult of Asklepius said, in a divine source. While the healer may mediate healing, the healer is not the source of healing. This humbling admission saves the humanity of the therapist and prevents him from assuming a godlike role, and also rescues the integrity and dignity of his client, who comes to realize that God speaks to him directly, and that health and wholeness lie within him and not within the therapist. The psyche is a self-healing organism, a remarkable totality that has the power to heal and renew itself. How the psyche heals itself, and what conditions are necessary for such healing to take place, are the concerns we will look at next.

Notes

1. Mircea Eliade, *Shamanism* (Princeton, N.J.: Princeton University Press, 1964), p. 36.

2. John G. Neihardt, *Black Elk Speaks* (Lincoln, Nebr.: University of Nebraska Press, 1961, originally published in 1932), chapter 3, "The Great Vision," p. 20.

3. Adrian K. Boshier, "African Apprenticeship," *Parapsychology Review*, p. 25.

4. *Ibid.*, pp. 25-26. I am grateful to the late Kieffer Frantz, M.D., for putting me in touch with this article. A few months before he died in 1975, Dr. Frantz shared this article with me. Its inclusion here is a small tribute to him and his dedicated work of healing.

5. See Sheldon B. Kopp, "A Time for Priests, A Time for Shamans," *Psychological Perspectives*, Vol. I, #1, Spring, 1970, p. 9. There is, however, another meaning to the priest. He is the one who deals with numinous (sacred) realities on behalf of the whole people. But this sense of priesthood is all but lost today, for the institution of the church stands between the priest and the Numinosum.

6. See Franc Johnson Newcomb, *Hosteen Klah* (Norman, Okla.: University of Oklahoma Press, 1964), pp. 27-29.

7. Robert Lindner, *The Fifty Minute Hour* (New York: Rinehart & Co., Inc., 1955).

V

Healing in the Psychology
of C. G. Jung

The most important contribution to healing in our century has come through the discovery of the unconscious, and the exploration of its far-reaching implications for our understanding of illness and health. Ever since Sigmund Freud, at the turn of the century, found it was possible to cure certain people of their symptoms through a purely psychological treatment, and in so doing demonstrated the reality of the unconscious, there has been a revolution in the mind of modern man. This revolution has affected our language, penal system, philosophy of life, religion, education and medicine. Psychological words such as "complex," "introvert," "extravert," "insight," and "repression" are common now in our language. Devices such as the polygraph (lie detector) are based upon the premise that there is an unconscious mind, and go back historically to C. G. Jung's Word Association Experiments. Doctors now take into account this same realm of unconscious mental and emotional functioning in the study of psychosomatic medicine, and focus increasingly on the interaction between physical illness and psychological processes of which their patients may be only dimly aware.

The discovery of the unconscious is really a rediscovery, for what we call the unconscious has been known by ancient people long before us. In the Bible, for instance, the unconscious is designated by the word "heart," which occurs in the Bible hundreds of times, never with reference to the physical organ of the heart, but as a synonym for a hidden, inner part of the personality. The word "soul" is another Biblical word that refers to the unconscious, inner man, and the sayings of Jesus, as I have shown in my book *The Kingdom Within*, reveal a knowledge on the part of Jesus of the hidden workings of the human mind. In primitive people, such as the American Indians, what we call today "the unconscious" is exteriorized in the spiritual world which was very real to these people, that realm of spirit-beings and autonomous powers that was believed to influence human life in a crucial way.

The reasons for modern Western man's loss of contact with the unconscious go beyond the scope of this book. Suffice it to say that as the church lost its interest in healing, and became more identified with institutional structure and doctrinal formulations, the living spirit of the soul disappeared and went underground. Somewhat later the attitude of rationalistic materialism—which rejects anything paradoxical, ambiguous, or obscure—and materialism—which declares that everything real must be known through the senses of the body—came to dominate the Western outlook on life, science, and religion, and resulted in a rejection of the inner world of man and his nonrational spiritual nature. So complete was this rejection that the rediscovery of the unconscious[1] by scientists like Freud and C. G. Jung was extraordinarily innovative, and came like a flash of lightning in the spiritual darkness of mankind.

In times past man's religion provided the link with the world of the unconscious. The inner realm of man was taken into account by man's religious outlook, and his mythology and cosmology were like charts of the soul. Once man lost this dimension to his religion he also lost contact with the unconscious. Rejected and separated from consciousness, the unconscious turned hostile and in our century has erupted in barbaric wars, crime, and the sickness of soul so characteristic of our times. The rediscovery of the unconscious makes it possible to establish a connection once more between the world of consciousness and the world within man. The difference is that modern man must understand the spiritual world as part of his own psychic structure, while primitive or ancient man projected it out into a world of supernatural beings and mythological forces.

Freud was able to make his discoveries because he had succeeded to a certain extent in freeing himself from the materialism and rationalism that had gripped the psychiatry of his time. The 19th century was the acme of determinism, that philosophy fostered by 19th century physics which saw the universe as a vast machine having fixed laws and moved by mechanical forces. The 19th century physicist believed that if he only knew enough of the forces at work in the universe he could successfully predict the entire course of cosmic events, for everything was determined. Psychiatry at that time had the same philosophy, and man was viewed as a little machine. Psychological disturbances were believed to be entirely organic in nature, and psychiatry contented itself with the classification of mental disturbances and the search for their physical causes, which, it was certain, must always exist.

Freud's genius was that he was sufficiently free of this deterministic thinking to perceive the autonomy of psychological processes and find a way to cure his patients by purely psychological means. Since this went counter to the prevailing attitudes of his profession his work met with great opposition from his medical and psychological colleagues; change is always resisted most by those who have the most to give up if they accept it. Nevertheless, Freud's work continued, and the truth in it eventually won a hearing. Out of this came the fundamental ideas of depth psychology: the unconscious, the theory of repression, the concept of psychic energy or libido, and, most important for our discussion, as we will see later, the discovery that healing occurs when unconscious contents are made conscious.

The difficulty with Freud's work was that he did not go far enough in freeing himself from the materialistic bias of his time. Ultimately Freud himself succumbed to materialism, and saw man as a biological animal, whose personality was an epiphenomenon of physical processes, no matter how autonomous his psychological processes might become. This limitation compelled Freud to see man's psychic energy in exclusively sexual terms, and to reduce all psychological phenomena to a supposed biological basis. This, of course, ruled out the spiritual dimension of man, and the symbolic function of the unconscious, and reduced the psyche to "nothing but" a representation in consciousness of physical processes. For this reason Freud's greatest successes came with patients whose problems centered on the repression of traumatic experiences with sexual overtones, but his psychology was unable to deal with personality disorders that had a broader and more spiritual basis.

Freud's concept of the unconscious limited it to the purely personal sphere. It was the repository of forgotten or repressed experiences and emotions peculiar to the individual, something like a basement into which disagreeable or unwanted things are thrown away and hidden. That there is such a dimension to the psyche is beyond a doubt, and where there are repressed experiences they do set up a disturbance of the conscious personality and its functioning. This, as Freud showed, can be alleviated by lifting the repression and reexperiencing the traumatic and troublesome episodes.

When repressed psychological material of this sort reaches consciousness it brings with it first a devastating, then, if properly integrated, a healing effect. A woman in her late thirties came for help because of depression and suicidal fantasies. Up to this point her adult life had been in order and without apparent psychological difficulty, but now she was acutely ill and suffering greatly. She felt on the brink of despair but without any apparent reason. We discussed her outer life situation but we could find no reason in this area for her depression. Her marriage seemed to be a good one, and she had two fine and healthy children. She had few dreams and only one made an impression. This was a dream in which her deceased mother entered a house into which the family had recently moved, walked solemnly through each room in it with a detached, ghostlike air, and left the house without saying a word. She could make no sense of the dream, since she remembered her mother only in a positive light, and could not account for the way her mother's "ghost" haunted her in the dream. She claimed her childhood had been a happy one, and that she loved her mother.

For many weeks we discussed her situation without any positive result. I felt increasingly alarmed, for her suicidal fantasies were very strong. It often seemed to me that we were making no progress whatsoever and the only thing to cling to was the relationship. Then one day, without any warning, she suddenly burst into a flood of tears. For twenty minutes she wept hysterically and seemed to be quite out of control. There was nothing I could do, for it was almost as though I was not even in the room. When the hysterical sobbing finally abated she was able to tell me what had happened.

She had been conversing with me about quite ordinary things when there had suddenly erupted into her consciousness a memory of an experience when she was about eleven years old. In this scene she was kneeling before her mother, who had a knife poised at her breast, pleading with her not to kill herself. This scene came back with enormous emotional force; it was as though she *was* the child again and the whole scene was being reenacted. With the return of this memory the dam broke and she was flooded by disturbing memories of her childhood which, it now turned out, was agonizingly painful because of her mother who was a disturbed woman who manipulated the children into doing what she wanted them to do through guilt. In the particular scene that had come back to her the mother was remembered as getting the child to do what she wished through threatening, in this bizarre manner, to commit suicide.

It was now clear that this woman's childhood was very unhappy, so emotionally tortured in fact that she had been enabled to get into life only by a repression of her childhood memories. It was as though nature had sealed off her unhappiness to protect her ego against the destructive memories of her childhood, much as the body seals off tuberculosis bacilli in the lung by enclosing them in calcium. This measure was helpful at the time of her youth, but if she was to become a complete person, her childhood had to come back into consciousness eventually, for our soul is not complete unless we are in possession of the whole of our lives, be it happy or unhappy. This meant that her childhood memories had to become conscious to her again, and their original emotional force reexperienced. Only in this way could her childhood psyche be redeemed and healed. In her talks with me it was as though a faucet had been turned on and the water left running. If that happens, water that is far underground to begin with will eventually reach the top and come pouring out. So it was with the repressed childhood memories. It is not surprising that this process was forced upon her as she got into middle life for that is the time when the clamor for individuation, and the demands of the unconscious for recognition, become most urgent.

*   *   *   *

This woman's story illustrates how healing can take place when repressed contents of the unconscious are made conscious. It also illustrates the self-healing nature of the psyche, demonstrated first in the sealing-off of the troublesome episodes from childhood, and later in the demand that they be made conscious again so she could become whole. None of this was initiated from consciousness, of course, but was the natural function of her psyche. From this it can be seen that the unconscious is not only like a basement into which things we do not want to face are discarded, but is also like a partner of the conscious personality, and embodies within it the wisdom and guidance of nature. It was this dimension of the psyche, overlooked by Freud, that was the main focus of interest for C. G. Jung.

Because Jung was free of the materialistic bias, he was able to approach the psyche without any assumptions about what it had to be like and so was able to observe it scientifically and impartially. Jung's ideas about the psyche came from two major sources: the psychological material that came from his patients, and his experience with his own unconscious. Jung paid careful attention to everything that came from his patients. No fantasy, dream, psychotic hallucination, or strange behavior was left unexamined. Meaning was looked for in everything. He also paid careful attention to everything that crossed his own mind, and his consciousness was often flooded by powerful images and affects from the unconscious. A lesser person than Jung might have broken under the impact of the unconscious when he underwent the transforming experiences he describes for us in chapter six in his autobiography *Memories, Dreams, Reflections*. Jung survived psychologically because he was able to make sense of what was happening to him, and he was able to help many of his patients in the same way. In this manner Jung developed his major ideas, and arrived at a certain understanding of the nature of illness and the means of cure.

The psyche, Jung realized, was not only a personal repository of undesirable psychological material, but was something like a 3,000,000 year old mind. Like the body, the psyche also is a product of a long evolution. Within the psyche is the stored-up wisdom of life as it has been expressed in man, and perhaps also man's humanoid predecessors, for millions of years. No one believes that he personally produces his body. We all recognize the instinctive wisdom of the body, its remarkable capacity for adjustment to the demands of life, and its ability to heal itself. It is the same way with the psyche, which likewise is self-healing, and contains an equally rich wisdom. Only the ego, the center of consciousness, is more or less limited in scope to the personal life history of the individual; the unconscious has its roots far back in time.

But the unconscious also extends into the future. At the same time that it seems to contain the stored-up wisdom of life as it has evolved over the millenia, so it also seems to contain a secret knowledge of life's goal. Everything that is alive seeks its proper goal, as we saw in chapter one, and man's psyche is no exception. The human body also seeks its proper goal. From the moment of conception the cells of the body "know," in a mysterious fashion, their goal, and the physical body unfolds until it reaches its completed development at about the age of seventeen. The psyche is no different, except that the development of the psyche is never completed, for the possibilities of life within us cannot be exhausted. It is as if evolution, which produced the human organism under the guidance of the divine spirit in nature, continues within each individual seeking to bring about the maximum development and consciousness. This is the nature of the psyche, and out of this come man's religious yearnings and his spiritual side, for the yearning for wholeness is the equivalent on the psychological plane of the yearning for God. This dimension of the unconscious, which transcends the individual in time and scope and extends far beyond the boundaries of the ego, Jung called the "collective unconscious."

The collective unconscious contains the world of the archetypes. The archetypes are *a priori*, preexisting patterns of energy within us. When something is archetypal it expresses itself in typical ways, which gives to human beings everywhere a certain common denominator and is the psychological basis for the idea of the brotherhood of man. The archetypes include what is called "instinct" because they are the basis for all spontaneous, unlearned behavior, but while we think of instinct in terms of physical drives and motor action, the archetype also expresses itself in imagery, emotion, and meaning. The archetype is like a spectrum of colors. On the one end is the physical expression of the archetype, the instinct, and on the other end of the spectrum is the *meaning* of the archetype, or spirit. In between is a vast range of images and emotions that, when the archetype is constellated within us, are released to flood our minds with energy.

Jung's discovery of the archetypes was the key to understanding the world of mythology, fairy tales, and dreams. Myths are like the clothing of the archetypes. In myths the archetypal, that is, typical, patterns underlying human life are depicted in a universal story form. The archetypal structure of the psyche accounts for the astonishing similarity of mytholigical motifs all over the world which Jung, Joseph Campbell, and others have demonstrated.[2] Fairy tales also are archetypal stories, and the witches, giants, and robber-barons of fairy tales personify the typical psychological dangers the ego must face on its way through life.

The archetypal structure of the psyche is also the basis of polytheistic religions. The gods and goddesses of ancient Greece can be understood as personifications of the archetypes. Aphrodite, the great goddess of lovemaking, and her mischievous son Eros, live again whenever human beings fall in love, or are possessed by the divine madness of sexual desire. Ares, too, god of war, personifies the archetypal energy for war and bloodlust that lies slumbering in the psyche of the most peaceful storekeeper among us until it is aroused by the beat of the war drum or the nearness of the enemy. So the psyche of man includes gods and goddesses, angels and demons, spirits and fabulous beings, and these make up what has been called "the savage and beautiful country" of the unconscious.[3]

Much of Jung's work consisted in describing the different archetypes of the collective unconscious. The shadow, for instance, is the dark side of the personality that each person carries, the unwanted or inferior person within us who contradicts our ideal image of ourselves and is as inevitably a part of us as Mr. Hyde was a part of Dr. Jekyll. The shadow must be faced if we are to become whole, and for this reason individuation sometimes seems to be one unpleasant revelation about oneself after another. The anima is another important archetype researched by Jung. It personifies the feminine element in a man. The nature of the anima is as complex as that of the goddesses of ancient man and she imbues a man's life with boundless complexities and entanglements. Conversely, the animus in a woman personifies her masculine side. Appearing to her either as devil or divine guide, the animus can crush a woman's soul in his grip or enrich her with all the possibilities of the world of spirit and meaning. But these archetypes, and many others, have already been described by Jung and his colleagues and fall beyond the scope of this book.

Man's polytheistic religion corresponds to the tremendous diversity in his psyche, but his inclination to monotheism springs from the Self, or psychic Center. This, as we saw before, is the archetype of unity, the centering tendency within us that unites the warring, conflicting elements of the psyche. It corresponds to an image of God in the human soul, and is the basis for the individuation process. Thus the Self is also the ultimate basis for healing, since becoming whole is being healed, and being healed means to become whole.

Clearly the unconscious for Jung is far more than it was for Freud. It is inexhaustible because its capacity for formulating new possibilities in life never comes to an end. Rather than being only like a basement into which things are discarded, and which could, theoretically, be exhausted by consciousness, the unconscious is like a vast inner world, and accompanies us throughout our lifetime as our enemy or our friend, our antagonist or our guiding angel, but, in any case, an indispensable partner in the healing process.

*   *   *   *

For psychological healing to occur there must be a relationship between the ego and the forces of the unconscious. This relationship is achieved primarily through becoming conscious of the contents of the unconscious. The psyche, as we have seen, naturally seeks wholeness, but this wholeness can only be achieved through the development of consciousness and the unfolding of the whole man in the given life-context of the individual. Thus wholeness results in the reorganization of the personality on a higher, more developed level. Since this kind of growth can never be achieved without the death of the old state of consciousness, there is, inevitably, in every instance in which someone begins to become whole, a considerable measure of pain and suffering. Indeed, as we saw in the case of shamanism, the death process that precedes all psychological and spiritual change may take the form of illness, which accounts in part for the curious relationship that exists between illness and health.

Whether or not the forces of the unconscious act on our behalf depends on our relationship to them. In ancient religions the gods and goddesses were exceedingly jealous. To win their favor man had to worship them and attend their temples with the appropriate sacrifices and devotions. To ignore them was to incur their wrath and revenge. In the Old Testament, Yahweh too was a jealous God, Who demanded great attention from mankind and was easily provoked when He was ignored. On the psychological level this means that we must pay due heed to each of the archetypal factors that make up our psyche. Anything rejected in the unconscious turns against us; on the other hand, to give conscious energy to the contents of the unconscious is to begin to win their positive energy and support.

For instance, a man who devalues the feminine side of himself and of life can expect revenge from the offended psychic powers. Aphrodite takes her revenge in many strange ways. The highly successful business or professional man, for instance, who devotes himself wholeheartedly to his masculine pursuits of power and success, and ignores the requirements of relationship, love, and eros, may be victimized by failures in marriage or compulsive sexual fantasies. A seemingly powerful and successful man-of-the-world may be seized by the urge to watch pornographic movies, or may be unable to relate to wife and family. In this way the goddess, that is, the archetype of the feminine, takes revenge for being ignored.

This is why the Self, which is our greatest friend, can also seem like our enemy. Our relationship to the Self will depend upon our relationship to the demands of individuation. To ignore these demands is to turn the forces of the unconscious against us. The sea of the unconscious then becomes dark, stormy, and threatening, like the sea in the fairy tale of the Fisherman and the Flounder.

The negative state of affairs that comes about when the unconscious is not included as a partner in life is often manifested in disturbing symptoms and troubled dreams. Cancer phobias and cancer dreams are good examples. Cancer is a condition in which cells are being multiplied but not integrated into the body; as a result they destroy it. When individuation begins, new life is continually being developed from the unconscious. If it is not integrated into the conscious personality it begins to grow against the personality, and the symptomatic expression of this may be a phobia of having cancer. People with this condition have been known to go from doctor to doctor, always convinced that they have the disease even though each physician assures them that they do not.

Fantasies or dreams of a threatened invasion are another common symptom of the malaise that results from a cleavage between the conscious and the unconscious personalities. When the unconscious appears as a threat to the ego it may be projected in the form of such a fear. This may be concretized in the form of fear of the Russians, the Chinese, or whoever the latest version of the "enemy" may be, or it may be more on the level of a fear of burglars breaking into the house. In dreams, men from outer space may land on earth creating great panic, or waves of primitive men may attack the dreamer. In such ways do dreams represent the disturbing conflict that has arisen between the conscious and unconscious personalities, but also hint that the unconscious wants to be integrated into consciousness, hence it "invades" the ego which, if the situation is to be dealt with correctly, must accept the demand of this inner world for inclusion and integrate it by becoming conscious of it.

*　*　*　*

Depth psychology has provided us with a model of the psyche that enables us to understand the meaning of many illnesses. Psychosis, for instance, when it is not due to possible organic causes, as may be the case in certain types of disintegrative schizophrenia, can be understood as an overwhelming of the ego by the forces of the unconscious. The unconscious expresses itself by exceedingly powerful images that are autonomous; that is, they have their own life and vitality. Ordinarily the ego is able to screen out these images of the unconscious sufficiently so that during waking hours we can function correctly, deal with the outer world, and keep a distinction between inner and outer reality. But in certain cases the inner images may be too strong, the defenses of the ego too weak, and the threatened invasion takes place in the form of a psychosis. In this state the difference between inner and outer reality is obscured. It is like living in a dream when awake: the "dream reality" is so strong that the individual loses the common psychological perspective of his fellows and becomes "crazy." This is especially likely to happen if the person is psychologically isolated from others; therefore an antidote to psychosis is human relatedness, though its ultimate cure will require an understanding of the meaning of the threatening, overwhelming images of the unconscious.

Psychosis is like being at the bottom of the ocean; other people are seen, but from the bottom of the sea one cannot reach out to them. Or it can be likened to being overwhelmed by a flood or great tidal wave, or consumed in a raging fire, symbolizing the way the naked affects, emotions, and images of the unconscious overwhelm the conscious personality. We speak of being "flooded with ideas," or

"drowning" in our emotions. The psychosis cannot be integrated if
the ego lacks the requisite understanding. A cure is possible, however,
if another human is able to relate to the ill person, and the contents of
the unconscious can be differentiated and understood. Then it can be
seen that what looked like an illness is actually a cure; that is, the
psychosis is really an attempt to cure that person of a maladjusted
ego. The original illness was an inadequate conscious development;
there was something wrong with that individual to begin with, some
maladjustment or psychological inadequacy. The flood of images
from the unconscious contains the cure. If correctly understood and
integrated, the images result in a change of personality that can lead
to greater health. So the flood of images that comes to someone during a psychosis can be understood as an attempt on the part of the
unconscious to cure him and set him on the path to wholeness.

Some people lie very close to the unconscious and live with a
constant threat of being overwhelmed by it. Others have, so to speak,
a solid wall around the ego and the images of the unconscious are
kept at a distance. These people will not even know what you are
talking about when you speak of the unconscious. Either person
labors under a psychological difficulty. In the first case the threatened
invasion can, as we have seen, lead to a seeming disaster. More
frequently the ego defenses are sufficiently strong to prevent the complete overwhelming of consciousness, but the price paid for keeping
out the threatened invasion is a crippling anxiety, or the feeling of living continually under a dark cloud. Such people may have the fear of
going insane, a good indication that they will not, since such a high
anxiety indicates an ego structure that resists being totally overwhelmed. In this case the task is to integrate the contents of the unconscious, and, in order to compensate for the overwhelming nature
of the inner images, reinforce reality factors of ordinary life adjustment. Given a good relationship with a therapist, and the capacity of
therapist and client to understand what is happening, the outlook is
hopeful, though a sense of humor helps too.

Jung offers us the following synopsis of these two complemen-
tary states of relationship that may exist between the ego and the
forces of the Self:

> "It must be reckoned a psychic catastrophe when the *ego is
> assimilated by the self*. The image of wholeness then re-
> mains in the unconscious, so that on the one hand it shares
> the archaic nature of the unconscious and on the other finds
> itself in the psychically relative space-time continuum that is

characteristic of the unconscious as such. Both these qualities are numinous and hence have an unlimited determining
effect on ego-consciousness, which is differentiated, i.e., separated, from the unconscious and moreover exists in an
absolute space and an absolute time. It is a vital necessity
that this should be so. If, therefore, the ego falls for any
length of time under the control of an unconscious factor,
its adaptation is disturbed and the way opened for all sorts
of possible accidents.

"Hence it is of the greatest importance that the ego should
be anchored in the world of consciousness and that consciousness should be reinforced by a very precise adaptation.
For this, certain virtues like attention, conscientiousness,
patience, etc., are of great value on the moral side, just as
accurate observation of the symptomatology of the unconscious and objective self-criticism are valuable on the intellectual side.

"However, accentuation of the ego personality and the
world of consciousness may easily assume such proportions
that the figures of the unconscious are psychologized and
the *self consequently becomes assimilated to the ego.* Although this is the exact opposite of the process we have just
described it is followed by the same result: inflation. The
world of consciousness must now be levelled down in favour
of the reality of the unconscious. In the first case, reality
had to be protected against an archaic, "eternal" and "ubiq-
uitous" dream-state; in the second, room must be made for
the dream at the expense of the world of consciousness. In
the first case, mobilization of all the virtues is indicated; in
the second, the presumption of the ego can only be damped
down by moral defeat. This is necessary, because otherwise
one will never attain that median degree of modesty which is
essential for the maintenance of a balanced state."[4]

We have already mentioned the young woman who came for
analysis when she was in danger of dissociation. Her first dream, we
saw, was that of a fiery ball that the dream said she could now take
into herself "bit by bit" with the help of the therapist. In addition to
the fact that this dream offered a good prognosis for the outcome of
the therapeutic work, it also showed how that work should proceed:

things from the unconscious should be dealt with bit by bit, a little at a time. The Self, represented by the ball of fire, could be broken up and taken into consciousness in small doses. In this way the danger of the ego's being totally overcome by the unconscious could be alleviated, and the task of individuation could safely begin. To take the whole ball of fire into oneself at one time would amount to being burned up; that is, consumed in affects, overwhelmed by a disastrous inflation, or even lost in a psychotic outbreak.

But those who are able to hold the unconscious off at a distance also have their psychological problems, one of which may be psychological sterility. The ego has no creativity of its own, but gets its creative and new life from the unconscious. If the unconscious is not allowed into consciousness at all, the ego tends to become rigid, narrow, and constricted. Such a person suffers from psychological cramps and life tends to become dull, for the whole point of it is being missed. Eventually symptoms may develop for this person too. Problem drinking may begin, chronic irritability, disturbances in relationships, and a variety of sexual compulsions may be symptoms that the unconscious has been too estranged from consciousness and has set up a dangerous counter-position.

*   *   *   *

In either case dreams can be exceedingly helpful, for in our dreams we are given images of our psychological situation that help orient the ego and enable it to integrate the unconscious. For every psychological state there is a corresponding image. Unless we have an image of our condition we are in the dark about it, and feel victimized by a chaos, depression, or anxiety that has swallowed us like an invisible dragon. To have an image of our condition changes all this and enables us to come into relationship with the forces that beset us all around.

A person who suffers from estrangement from the unconscious is also helped by dreams because the dreams, via their imagery, permit contents of the unconscious to cross over into consciousness. There is also another helpful aspect to dreams: the fact that they bring up only what can now be integrated. Like the body of Christ, which is broken up so each individual can take a tiny portion at the Eucharist, so the Self is broken up into tiny bits by the dreams, and no more is offered at any one time than the individual can absorb.

In either case, changes are absolutely necessary. There is no wholeness without change, and change, as we have seen, is a matter of death and renewal. The "dying" process can be exceedingly frightening for, after all, if it is an authentic experience, one cannot be sure of the renewal to follow. All the ego often knows is that it is being forced to give itself up, and that is frightening indeed; sometimes only the faith of the therapist sees a person through such a psychological death experience.

This deep fear is often reflected in fantasies or dreams of the end of the world indicated perhaps by an invasion from outer space, or a gigantic storm. This state of affairs may even be projected into a religious fantasy system of the end of the world. In this case people are protected from a possible psychosis because a number of them share the same fantasy. If a person projects the contents of the unconscious into a metaphysical system of some sort, it becomes essential to get others to believe in that system too; otherwise one goes crazy with it. If no one had believed Adolph Hitler he would have been crazy, and so would many a religious reformer. This is what made Jesus so beautiful as a teacher; he had no metaphysical system to offer, but taught basic matters of the soul through the images of the parables. Thus we know that he had a true religious spirit.

Psychological change also requires the end of our "participation mystique," an unconscious identification with other people. When we live in such an identification, we do not have our own individual personalities, nor our personal relationship with the unconscious, but we have a group ego, so to speak. We are "at one" with other people. The group may be our family, our church, our fraternal organization, the military organization, etc. It is what Fritz Kunkel called "tribal psychology" as contrasted with individual psychology.

During youth this is a natural state of affairs. The young person needs such collective identification for it is too much to expect an individual relationship with the unconscious at this age. Identification with the football team, the group of peers, or a religious collective may be an aid to ego development at this time. But if individuation is to occur this must eventually be given up. Such psychological separation from others is painful. It results in a certain feeling of isolation and loneliness.

Paradoxically, however, only when participation mystique ends is true relatedness possible. Until then we have simply shared with others the same ego needs, group ego supports, and psychological defenses. Human relatedness at its highest level occurs when two *individuals* meet. The difficulty is that when one person begins to develop psychologically he or she cannot relate to others in the old, unconscious way. If this occurs in marriage there may be great stress in the marriage, for the development of one marriage partner will change the relationship and demand the development of the other partner as well, so that the whole relationship may evolve. Thus there is a certain amount of loneliness to individuation, as well as a developed capacity for relationship in depth.

There are a number of sayings of Jesus that speak of the necessity to end this state of participation mystique. Speaking of our unconscious identification with family Jesus says, for instance, "If any man comes to me without hating his father, mother, wife, children, brothers, sisters, yes and his own life too, he cannot be my disciple." (Luke 14:25) The word "hate" which Jesus uses is a very strong word, not meant to be taken literally, but indicating the intensity of our need to separate psychologically from those to whom we are the closest if we are to develop our own personalities.

If the demand from the unconscious for change is resisted too long fantasies of suicide may be the result as the unconscious urges that the old ego die so that a new life may evolve. If these death fantasies are not understood symbolically, they may be acted out and suicide attempts may result. This is especially likely to occur in people who are childish in their attitude and want attention and sympathy rather than creative change, or in cases in which there is unexpressed aggression, for suicide is also an aggressive act that hurts others because it brings about rejection and guilt. This is all a way of saying that there is a very dark side to the demand from within for wholeness, and if this inner demand is not properly met one may encounter the "wrath of God," which is the anger of life because it has been refused.

* * * *

To accept the unconscious as a partner in life is like letting in both God and the devil. The numinous energy of the unconscious, its power to move us toward wholeness, and its unfathomable intelligence and wisdom, give us the impression that the unconscious is the carrier of divine grace. But it also proves a devilish companion, and to allow its images, fantasies, and dreams into our consciousness is much like making a Faustian pact with the underworld. This is because the unconscious brings with it the dark, inferior part of our personality. All that is within us that we fear, and that is not developed because it seems morally ambiguous, emerges when the unconscious is accepted. Nor is there any way to bargain with the unconscious that only one side will appear and not the other. When it comes into consciousness the whole of the unconscious emerges, with its many and complex demands, and its devilish as well as divine qualities. To deal with the unconscious is thus to ask God into one's life and, at the same time, to have to come to terms with what appears to be the devil, that is, with the inferior and rejected side of one's personality.

It is because of its devilish aspect that the unconscious has a dubious reputation. Instinctively we sense its threatening and paradoxical qualities, and it is not surprising that its very existence is usually denied as long as possible so that only the injured, who must turn to it for help, or the very curious allow it in. We find ourselves rejecting the unconscious as the origin of dark things, especially if we possess a one-sided Christian consciousness that insists upon absolute goodness, and cannot tolerate the ambiguous and paradoxical side to wholeness.

To deny the existence of the inner world, however, is not to escape its devilish aspects, but rather to fall victim to them unknowingly, and this is when evil can enter in. Evil gains power when its existence is denied, or when we have become used to it and no longer are aroused by it. To deny the reality of the unconscious is not to know oneself, and not to know oneself is to risk becoming possessed by that which we have ignored. The more split-off from consciousness, and therefore from wholeness, something is, the more malignant it will act. This is clear from our dreams in which split-off parts of personality, such as the shadow, appear at first as threatening figures, but, if a relationship with them is established, later become our companions.

Possession by the unconscious takes place in direct relationship to our psychological ignorance of ourselves. We are most taken over, therefore, by what we do not recognize and understand. To deny the existence of the devil within us is to invite possession by him. For this reason, all manner of evil is perpetrated in the name of good, and fantastic forms of deviltry have been done in the name of God. In our time, possession by the shadow is a great danger. To live out our darkest urges compulsively and unconsciously is to become possessed by evil. Faced as we are in our time of history with a breakdown in moral attitudes, which no one admits is true of himself but only happens in other people, plus a denial of the unconscious, the shadow aspects of human nature are running rampant. The violence of our wars, the increase of crime, greed, the lust for power that has taken over our highest political offices, and the destruction of our environment all attest to our possession by the shadow. Yet if the origin of these things could be seen in *ourselves* this could all change and the dark powers within us could take their proper place in our whole personality. Morality extends only within the boundaries of consciousness. What we do not know about ourselves is not subject to our moral values, and moral standards and self-knowledge must go hand in hand. For this reason, in spite of its admittedly devilish aspect, the unconscious must be allowed into consciousness so that a life of the highest value may be attained, and the truly moral life lived.

Herein lies the danger of an overly simplistic attitude toward evil. On the one hand, there is the danger from the humanist and rationalist who is inclined to take too sanguine a view of human nature and overlook its deep propensity toward evil. On the other hand, there is the danger from certain religious groups that, while they take evil seriously, insist on projecting it in the form of a devil with a metaphysical status. There is, of course, an archetypal foundation to evil, and such a thing as naked evil really exists, but the difficulty with too much talk of the devil as an outer metaphysical being is that one's own devils get projected out. Then we never come to terms with the fact that *we* are angel and devil, and that the real struggle with evil begins with our manful wrestling with our own dark side. To do anything less than this is to overidentify with one side or the other. If we identify with the dark side of our nature, we are convinced we are beyond the reach of salvation, or, if our conscience is less sensitive, we act it all out. If we identify with the light side of our nature, we have too positive a view of ourselves, and see God as our ally against an unbelieving world. We then become like Joseph in Emily Brontë's novel *Wuthering Heights* whom she described as "the wearisomest self-righteous pharisee that ever ransacked a Bible to rake the promises to himself, and fling the curses on his neighbours."

* * * *

The psyche, as we have seen, is self-healing, and even an acute psychosis, which seems to be the illness itself, may actually be an attempt on the part of the psyche to reorganize a personality on a higher level.[5] What is true of a psychosis is also true of that psychological state called neurosis. A neurosis can be defined as a one-sidedness or malfunctioning of the ego that results in the crippling and constriction of life. Looked at in this way we all suffer from a neurosis, for no one can claim an ego state so perfected that the life of the whole person is not constricted; however, usually we reserve this term for those psychological conditions in which the constriction of life is so pronounced that it is obvious to us, or at least to those around us.

One measure of neurosis is to ask ourselves, "How does this psychological condition affect my life?" A sports writer suffered from fear of flying, yet his work often required him to fly to various cities to write on differing sports events. Since he was afraid to fly he thought of excuses and substitutions for doing this, but his work was constricted because of his anxiety. A successful analysis cured him of this phobia and his professional life was greatly expanded as a result. For another person fear of flying might not affect the way life is lived at all, or only very slightly, but chronic, groundless fears and anxieties over physical health might result in a useless and debilitating expenditure of time and energy in seeing doctors and taking medicines. Still others might be driven by neurosis to overdrinking, overeating, or some other form of compulsive behavior. Sexuality also can become neurotic; if sexual desires become overly compulsive our lives can be run by them, although the deep need they express is never satisfied.

Wherever there is a neurosis there is a compulsion at work, and compulsion is a demonstration par excellence of the reality of the unconscious. We all have compulsion in our lives, of course, but when the compulsion is so strong and so at variance with consciousness that it distresses us and confuses our lives it can be said to be the result of a neurotic dissociation. The usual attempt is to "get rid" of the unwanted compulsion, but in fact the compulsion is an attempt to heal us of our one-sidedness, and to call attention to something within us that has been neglected, to the detriment of our development. Jung says of this:

> "What the patient encounters in a neurotic dissociation is a strange, unrecognized part of his personality, which seeks to compel his recognition in exactly the same way that any other part of the body, if obstinately denied, would insist on its presence . . ."[6]

This statement sheds light on some of the underlying meaning of sexuality. Sexuality is an enormously complex psychological and spiritual matter, for the physical urges combine with the most delicate matters of love, personal relationship, and spiritual energy. There is, moreover, an important symbolic meaning to sexuality which shows that the object of our sexual desires stands in a secret relationship to our state of conscious development, and that something from the unconscious insists, through sexuality, upon recognition. In brief, the object of our sexual desires symbolizes what is lacking in our conscious development, and what we therefore "crave" in order to become complete beings. So we long for what we lack, and there is a compensatory relationship between the object of our sexual desires and fantasies and where we are in our conscious development.

Thus a heterosexually oriented man desires union with a woman; his masculine ego development needs to be compensated by inclusion of the feminine element. The situation, of course, is the reverse with women. In a homosexual man it is the masculine development that has not been properly completed, so a masculine object or person is the center of desire. Both heterosexual and homosexual fantasies, however, are never simple matters. It may not be just any woman who is the object of our desire, but a particular kind of woman, or a woman dressed in a particular way, and this too will have its special meaning. A man whom Edward C. Whitmont describes in his book *The Symbolic Quest* (New York: G. P. Putnam's Sons, 1969) was, for instance, unable to achieve an erection with a woman until he first kissed her feet. Whitmont showed that this man's masculine, logos development had far outstripped his appreciation of the feminine. He literally had to "lower his head" before he could achieve sexual union, in this way symbolically compensating for his exaggerated mental development and conscious devaluation of the feminine.

Similarly, with homosexual fantasies it may be the figure of a beautiful young man who arouses desire, or the longing for the male penis. In the former case this may occur as a compensation for an ego development that is too intellectual and devoid, therefore, of the living spirit and of eros. What has to be integrated is the androgynous "winged youth" and this image is projected onto a suitable young man who becomes the object of sexual desire. In the case of the penis, what is lacking is masculine power or creativity and this lacking element appears in projected form as the longing to embrace the penis. As long as the energy of the unconscious that lies behind our sexual fantasies and desires is experienced only in sexuality, its symbolic meaning is overlooked; hence the energy is not integrated and no significant changes take place in personality. We need not only to be in touch with our sexuality and able to express physical desires, but also we need to be able to understand their underlying symbolic meaning.

Looked at in this light neurosis can be seen as a psychological conflict, half of which has been repressed, and it is the repressed, denied factor that demands attention and recognition. The denial of this part of ourselves causes an inner conflict that eventually impairs our ego functioning. The answer to neurosis, therefore, is to make the conflict conscious. The inner war then emerges into the open and is accepted by us consciously. When this happens we are in a position to learn from the neurosis, and our conscious attitudes and development are changed so that the rejected, denied aspect of the personality can now be included in our development and in our lives. Jung says of this:

> "We should not try to 'get rid' of a neurosis, but rather to experience what it means, what it has to teach, what its purpose is. We should even learn to be thankful for it, otherwise we pass it by and miss the opportunity of getting to know ourselves as we really are. A neurosis is truly removed only when it has removed the false attitude of the ego. We do not cure it—it cures us. A man is ill, but the illness is nature's attempt to heal him. From the illness itself we can learn so much for our recovery, and what the neurotic flings away as absolutely worthless contains the true gold we should never have found elsewhere."[7]

It is for this reason that relating to the unconscious is a learning process. The unconscious has much to teach us, and to accept a relationship with it is to be taught by it. This is reflected in the many dreams in which we are in a classroom, or at a university, or have to take a test. The unconscious knows what we do not know and what we must learn about ourselves and life if we are to become well. To allow the repressed part of our personality into consciousness is to be taught what we need to know in order to become whole, and in this lies the cure.

In certain cases, especially where there is sexual energy involved, the presenting symptom does not yield quickly. The teaching goes on and on and the symptom remains as long as there is anything to be learned from it. Only in simple cases does a symptom yield its meaning rather quickly. A young married woman came to analysis because of a compulsive fantasy of murdering her husband. She had been married about two years to a fine young man whom she believed she loved greatly, so she was frightened to find herself possessed by a fantasy of murdering him with a knife while he slept. In the very act of seeing and loving him, this dark fantasy would possess her and the resulting conflict was, understandably enough, deeply disturbing to her. A brief history revealed that while she was happy to be married to her young husband, she had felt compelled to give up her own education and hopes for a career in an artistic field. When her husband moved to a different city to find new work she dutifully gave up her own educational goals and accepted the role of housewife. She enjoyed this, and yet something was lacking. "Is this all there is ever going to be?" she found herself asking as she tended to their house. Something in her was being denied in her otherwise idyllic marriage, and this part of her was calling attention to itself in a violent manner via the fantasies. As a result of our conversations the young woman decided that she must return to school and continue her own artistic pursuits. To her surprise her husband was agreeable to this. The fears she had that he would disapprove were not founded, and the thoughts she had in her mind that she could not do this came from her and not from him. Upon her decision to return to school and pursue her own career development, as well as be a wife, the dark fantasies ceased. She had learned what she was to learn and her neurosis disappeared.

*   *   *   *

The above story also shows that the meaning of an illness lies in the present. Even in cases in which the disturbing factor stems from repressed experiences from previous years, the disturbance still exists in the here-and-now and the cure lies in changing our attitudes in our present life and situation. Jung writes:

> "The true reason for a neurosis always lies in the present, since the neurosis exists in the present. It is definitely not a hangover from the past; . . . it is fed and as it were new-made every day. And it is only in the today, not in our yesterdays, that the neurosis can be 'cured.' Because the neurotic conflict has to be fought today, any historical deviation is a detour, if not actually a wrong turning."[8]

Bringing the unconscious into consciousness produces a cure; this is the main contribution of depth psychology to our knowledge of healing. In the case of a neurosis, as we have seen, a cure is wrought when the repressed portion of our psychological conflict becomes conscious to us. This does not mean, however, that our pain and tension necessarily disappear, but simply that the conflict no longer cripples us. It is the task of the ego to carry the burden of psychological conflict in life. To be human is to be in conflict and there is no escape from this. Not everything in the psyche is compatible with everything else. One tendency within us wars against another. Add to this the fact that the demands of the Self and the demands of the outer world may not be in accord, and it is clear that one cannot expect to live life free of conflict. It is almost certain, in fact, that the inner demands of the unconscious will conflict with the demands, expectations, and rules of others around us, and society in general. A friend of mine once remarked, "God is not very practical." Similarly, the demand placed upon us by one part of the psyche may conflict with another. Our capacity for rage or aggression will likely conflict with our yearning for peace or standards of loving, ethical behavior. Our sexual urges will not necessarily be compatible with our spiritual yearnings and aspirations.

Often this state of affairs is reflected in our dreams by two women—or two men—who are opposed to each other. In masculine dreams two women who conflict with each other may appear in a single dream, each wanting the man's attention, and the presence of the two women causes the man in the dream anxiety and concern. The two women personify two forces within him pulling him in different directions, perhaps one a "Hera" figure who calls him to the values of hearth and home, and the other an "Aphrodite" who calls him to adventures out of the home. The gods and the goddesses, we will remember, did not always get along either, and Hera and Aphrodite in particular disliked each other intensely. In women there may be two men who are opposed to each other in this way, one man perhaps personifying an adaptation to husband and social values, and the other personifying the call from the woman's own soul to her individual development. These things are not easily reconciled.

When the inner figures and urges are not recognized as aspects of the Self, but are projected onto people outside of us, such psychological conflicts are concretized in relationships. A married minister found that he fell in love with various women in his parish. Wherever he went this happened to him and caused great confusion in his family and professional life. In this case, the "other woman" of his erotic fantasies stood on the side of his personal, individual psychological development, while his wife personified his adaptation to the secure values of home and church. As long as he was not able to make this inner conflict conscious he was doomed to live it out on the outside, which damaged him and others greatly and did not lead to a resolution of the problem.

A good example from literature of the conflict of opposites in women is found in Emily Brontë's novel *Wuthering Heights* from which we quoted earlier. The heroine, Cathy, finds herself torn between two men: the gentle, refined, cultivated Edgar Linton, and the

fiery, passionate, gypsy-like Heathcliff. The first offers her a beautiful home, an assured place in society, and the role of wife-mother
that will not demand too much from her and will bring her comfort-
ing rewards. The second wants her very soul in relationship. Linton
personifies the pull within her toward social and conventional adaptation and the values of a cultured life, while Heathcliff personifies her
connection to her own wild soul and the demands of the unconscious
for psychological development. Both demands, and both sides of life,
have their place, but the two conflict dreadfully. Cathy tries to escape
her dilemma by marrying Linton, but Heathcliff returns to excite and
torment her. Because she is not mature enough to accept this conflict
of opposites, she is ultimately destroyed, for Heathcliff, restless and
ruthless as life itself, will not allow her to live in peace.[9]

The stuff of life is made out of such struggles. The path to
wholeness requires us to understand these conflicts and accept the
task of uniting the form of heaven with the energy of hell, as William
Blake once put it. We are cured of our malfunctioning, but are not
allowed "peace of mind" or "adjustment," for there is no growth in
that. In the language of Jesus, the path of individuation is the way of
the cross, the conscious carrying of the burden of our own psyche
with its opposing tendencies. "If anyone wants to be a follower of
mine, let him renounce himself and take up his cross every day and
follow me," Jesus says (Luke 9:23) and elsewhere he adds, "Do not
suppose that I have come to bring peace to the earth: it is not peace I
have come to bring, but a sword." (Mt. 10:34)

*   *   *   *

Optimum psychological health occurs when the ego completely
represents the Self, for then the whole range and potentiality of the
personality is expressed in consciousness. As we have seen, this ideal
state cannot ever be realized perfectly, but only approximated. There
is never a time, Jung notes, when we are not contradicted somewhere
from within, if for no other reason than that life continually changes
and so requires an ever-new adaptation if it is to be correctly expressed and lived. For this reason, the key to psychological health
does not lie in achieving a certain state of consciousness and holding
on to it, but in achieving a relationship to one's Self. This is accomplished by forging a relationship between the conscious and the
unconscious parts of the personality. For this to occur there must be
some way in which the unconscious is recognized, its validity accepted, and its contents and potentialities made conscious.

The process of becoming whole is thus like a cooperative effort between the ego and the unconscious. On the one hand, the ego needs the unconscious in order to be cured of its one-sidedness and malfunctioning. On the other hand, without the ego and its capacity for becoming conscious the inner development cannot take place. This dual relationship shows up in our dreams. Sometimes we are sick or ill, perhaps in a hospital or in need of a doctor, and in this way the dream expresses the maladaptation of the ego. But in other cases figures of the unconscious may come to us asking for help as if *we* were the doctor, expressing the need of the unconscious to be recognized by the ego.

To make something conscious is not an intellectual act as such, though certain intellectual constructs and theoretical ideas may prove useful tools in helping us grasp unconscious contents. The contents of the unconscious are never really integrated, however, until they have been experienced on an emotional level. In fact, the hardest people to help sometimes are intellectuals, for their intellect often stands in the way of a living, emotional relationship to the unconscious. They are also likely to be people who are the most identified with certain attitudes or philosophical or theological assumptions that must be given up. The more someone has to give up, the more resistant he is to accepting the perspective of the unconscious. To make something conscious requires all of our functions. The unconscious needs to be perceived intuitively, sometimes apprehended even sensually; its power needs to be felt, and its contents need to be correctly understood.

To make the unconscious conscious is an act of redemption. Redemption means to win something back from an imperfect to a perfect condition. What needs to be redeemed is the whole man, and, specifically, those parts of the personality that have been left out of life. When these split-off parts of the personality first appear in personality disturbances, dreams, or fantasies, they often have a bizarre or disturbing effect. In our dreams they may appear as a wild man or woman, as someone mentally ill, a criminal, a retarded child, or in animal form. Such figures clamor for redemption, and this requires that they be made conscious, a painful and disturbing task, but one that rewards us ultimately with new energy for life.

Why making something conscious changes the psychological situation is a mystery. Often people say of something they see in themselves, "But what do I *do* with it?" This may be an important question, for sometimes what we see in ourselves does demand a direct active expression in life, but very often becoming conscious constitutes in itself a redemptive act, changing the inner situation, and in-

tegrating the contents of the unconscious by bringing them into relationship with consciousness. Relationship is the key word. The
contents of the inner world ask to be related to the ego by being made
conscious. As we have seen, it is their rejection that causes the disturbance.

It was because he saw the importance of psychological consciousness in the process of redemption that Jung valued Gnosticism.
Gnosticism was an ancient religious system which taught that man
was redeemed by becoming conscious of his true spiritual origins, his
situation in the world, and his relationship to God. Some men, the
Gnostics claimed, carried within themselves a spark of the divine nature that had fallen from the spiritual world above and had become
caught in the material world below. These men must redeem themselves, and the Godhead, by escaping from their imprisonment in the
material world and rejoining the world of pure spirit above. To do
this they had to understand their true nature and situation, which
they were ignorant of to begin with, and this was made possible
because the upper, spiritual world had sent a divine emissary, the
Nous or Mind of God, to teach mankind what it needed to know.
Equipped with this knowledge, and knowledge of the secret passwords
and other occult lore necessary to make passage from the lower to the
upper realms, the spiritual men could hope for reunion with God.

The name "Gnosticism" comes from the Greek word "gnosis"
which means special, revealed knowledge. For a time gnostic elements were included in Christianity, and Christian theologians such
as Clement of Alexandria and Origen termed themselves Christian
gnostics, that is, "Christians-in-the-know." But eventually the tension
between faith (pistis) and knowledge (gnosis), and other doctrinal differences, forced a split between the main stream of Christianity and
Gnosticism.

Along with the rejection of Gnosticism went the rejection by
Christianity of its original emphasis upon consciousness and illumi-
nation as a way to the knowledge of God, an emphasis clearly present, for instance, in the Gospel of John, where there is much discussion of light and darkness, seeing and not seeing. Because the value of
becoming conscious has been denied by the prevailing religious attitude of our time, as exemplified in the institutionalized churches, it
has reappeared in the unconscious, which now demands that we come
to "know." This emphasis is reflected in the many dreams in which
light plays an important role. We turn on the light switch, the head-
lights on our car do not work, we find ourselves walking along a dark
road at night, or it is the dawn of a new day. Even our language talks

of the importance of light for we say "it dawned upon me," meaning that we became conscious of something we did not know before. Jesus, of course, frequently stressed the importance of light symbolism in sayings such as, "the lamp of the body is the eye. It follows that if your eye is sound, your whole body will be filled with light. But if your eye is diseased, your whole body will be all darkness. If then, the light inside you is darkness, what darkness that will be!" (Mt. 6:22-23).

* * * *

The healing relationship between the ego and the unconscious requires that we accept a certain state of tension. Both the ego and the unconscious have their values and both must be respected. As mentioned before, the ego has the task of relating to both the outer and the inner worlds. Each has its demands and no one can say for certain when one must give way to the other. There are no rules one can rely upon, and no fixed standards where security can be found. The task of becoming whole is accomplished by the relationship between the conscious world and the unconscious world and the nature of this relationship will be different with each person.

Jung likened this relationship to an *auseinandersetzung*, a German word meaning a running dialogue between one reality and another. In this auseinandersetzung the position of the ego cannot just be given up, no matter how inadequate it may appear to be, nor can the demands of the unconscious be excluded. Sometimes the only answer for the ego on its island of consciousness is to negotiate with the unconscious and try to work something out. Speaking of the therapist's role in this process, Jung writes:

> "The doctor is well aware that the patient needs an island and would be lost without it. It serves as a refuge for his consciousness and as the last stronghold against the threatening embrace of the unconscious. The same is true of the normal person's taboo regions which psychology must not touch. But since no war was ever won on the defensive, one must, in order to terminate hostilities, open negotiations with the enemy and see what his terms really are. Such is the intention of the doctor who volunteers to act as a mediator. . . . He knows that the island is a bit cramped and that life on it is pretty meagre and plagued with all sorts of imaginary wants because too much life has been left outside,

and that as a result a terrifying monster is created, or rather
is roused out of its slumbers. He also knows that this seemingly alarming animal stands in a secret compensatory relationship to the island and could supply everything that the
island lacks."[10]

In this matter of negotiating with the unconscious, first one side
and then the other must be acknowledged, for life always seems to
have two sides to it. A young man came to me because of his inability
to study at school. Although he had been a gifted student in college
he now found that he was failing in law school; in fact, he showed all
the signs of a mental collapse. He could not concentrate, he could not
read, he was torn with sleeplessness and constant anxiety. He complained that when he tried to study he would read the same sentence
ten times and still not understand what it meant. There was one indication, however, that his mental condition was not as impaired as it
might seem. "One day," he related, "I found I could not retain anything I was reading in my law books. But I had a book by C. G. Jung
nearby and, despairingly, I thought, 'I will look at that for a while.'
Three hours later I was still reading it and realized that I had understood everything that it said."

It seemed clear from this that there was nothing wrong with his
mind, but something in him was vigorously rebelling against his intended career in law. On the other hand, to terminate his law studies
would be difficult. He had already invested a year in the program, his
influential father was putting pressure on him to finish, he was in the
middle of the semester, if he quit law school he would forfeit
hundreds of dollars of tuition, and he had no other prospects in life. It
was simply not practical to stop his studies, but nonetheless the day
after our appointment he went to the dean of the school and resigned.
Overnight his symptoms vanished; his anxiety was gone, his concentration returned, he could read and retain everything. He was cured,
for the demands of the unconscious had been satisfied. In this case
"negotiation" meant the ego's complete capitulation to his inner
voices, which clearly had something in mind for him other than law.

However, he now had other difficulties. He had no money, and
no other pursuit in life to follow. The only thing in life that seemed
interesting to him was the study of psychology, but first he had to
find himself in the world and earn the money to return to school. So
off he went to Alaska where he was fortunate enough to get a high-
paying job. One would think the unconscious would have respected
his need to earn money, even though the work he was doing was not

suited to his ultimate life goals, but he continued to suffer great tension and anxiety and could only get relief by paying assiduous attention to his dreams. This time, however, he pursued his work and saved his money and did not yield to the objections being voiced from within. In his negotiations with the unconscious he had first capitulated his ego goals in favor of the desires of the unconscious; the second time he insisted that the demands from within had to be delayed for a time while he solved the reality problems of jobs and money.

Jung, in the quotation we just read, mentions the doctor "who volunteers to act as a mediator." In Jungian psychotherapy this is the role that the therapist often plays. The client comes with a psychological situation in which the conscious and the unconscious parts of the personality are at variance, and the therapist tries to mediate between the two. In performing this role, the understanding the therapist has of the unconscious may be extremely important. It may prove to be the only light in what is otherwise total darkness, because in the beginning the client usually lacks an understanding of the nature of his conflicts. This is not only because the client may not be trained in such matters, but also because we are all lost in the trees of our own forest. It is hard for the best-trained person to see himself clearly because he is in the midst of his own situation which encompasses him on every side in a most confusing manner. This is why having another person in our lives, be it a professional therapist, a spiritual director, or an informed friend, is almost essential for those who seek wholeness.

In addition to his knowledge, the therapist also gives his client energy via his interest in the client's life situation, and this not only supports and encourages his client but, so to speak, helps create a container, formed by the relationship between the two of them, in which the contents of the psyche may be held. Since the therapist can take his client no further than he himself has gone, the therapist's own individuation is of crucial importance. It is not so much what the therapist does that matters, but who he is. The healing that ensues comes from two sources: first, the healing that lies in the unconscious of the client, that is, the self-healing powers of his own psyche that are released by increasing psychological awareness. Second, the effect on the client of the personality of the therapist. This is so important that it can be said that healing takes place via the interaction of the two people. For this reason it is extremely important that the therapist shall have undergone his own analysis, and, in fact, be continually in touch with his own psyche. It would be too much to expect the therapist to be "individuated," that is, completed as a person. He too is simply a human being trying to make his way through the world, but it is essential that he be in the midst of his own process of development, or else he cannot relate to that of his client. Perhaps the best motivation that he can bring to his work is that he must do it in order to maintain his own health and growth. If he adopts a superior attitude toward his client, and acts in a godlike, know-it-all way, he will only keep his client in an inferior, ill position. "All health to the therapist, all illness to the patient," does not work a cure, but only perpetuates two forms of illness: the acknowledged illness of the client, and the hidden illness of the therapist.

The situation will be difficult enough as it is, for the client will almost certainly project onto the therapist the archetype of the Self or the healer, and if the therapist identifies with this and comes to believe in his own magical qualities, all is lost. The antidote to this is the modest admission on the part of the therapist that he is compelled to help people because otherwise his life would be unfulfilled. The initiation of the shaman to the healing vocation applies in our day too, and the therapist who has come to the healing arts through his own illness and his own need to find a cure has the best spiritual preparation for the work of a healer.

The therapist acts as an outside mediator, but his intervention would be of no avail if it were not for the natural tendency of the psyche to heal itself by reconciling the unconscious and the conscious points of view. The great mediator of our psychic conflicts is within, and begins to work in us as soon as the symbols of the unconscious are recognized and accepted by us as part of our inner reality. Such an acceptance allows the natural mediating power of the Self to operate, thereby producing the possibility for a reconciliation of the opposites, and the emergence of a hitherto unconscious totality. This symbol-making aspect of the unconscious is called by Jung the "transcendent function" because it enables the psyche to transcend the conflict of the opposites, and permits consciousness to move out of a previously limited condition and emerge into a new life and vitality. If it were not for this transcendent function we could never emerge from one state to another, but would remain caught forever in a limited and constricted psychology. For this reason the symbols and images of the unconscious, produced by dreams, fantasies, and spontaneous images, are of crucial importance in the healing process.

The true healing, reconciling factor in us is this God-given function of the Self, but since the therapist also functions somewhat in this mediating role, he may become the carrier of the Self-image for the client. This makes the healing relationship a very delicate one. Misunderstandings will immediately cloud it and must be quickly worked out; the therapist must be free to admit his own responsibility in them and not put his client in the position of always being in error. The therapist must remain in touch with his own humanness and should never conceal this from his client via a professional persona or by playing a role. By simply being himself in the situation, and not afraid to be fully human, the chances are increased that the projection of the Self that he carries can ultimately be withdrawn, and the client can realize that he carries the seeds of his own healing and creativity.

Unconscious contents, such as the Self or the creative animus or anima, which have been projected onto the therapist or vice versa, must be made conscious wherever possible. This can be difficult, for these projected factors are often not seen and a healing relationship may endure for quite a while without their being visible. I recall one young man with whom I worked for a couple of years who finally, in response to an obvious error I made with regard to understanding his life situation, suddenly declared, "Then you are *not* omniscient!" This was the first I knew that he had regarded me as omniscient. To the contrary, he had been a rather argumentative client, not at all inclined to accept everything I said or suggested on the basis of my supposed authority. My error came to him with the force of a revelation. On my part it was welcome, not only because it had the effect of returning to him the archetype of the Self, but because it relieved me of the burden of having to carry the image of totality for him.

In another situation a woman who was very nervous about a forthcoming visit with her daughter, with whom she had had a troubled relationship for years, finally prevailed upon me to give her some advice. Suggestions are one thing, but advice is another, and it is usually nonproductive or destructive. As a rule, advice, even when assiduously sought, is disregarded, and if it is followed it often proves wrong. So it was in this case, and the woman returned from her visit very angry because she had followed my advice and it had turned out badly and led to a fruitless argument. After listening carefully to her anger at my stupidity, something prompted me to say, "Well, that's what you get for following my advice." Fortunately her sense of humor saved us both and our relationship survived my bad advice and my outrageous statement. She never asked for my advice again, and found she could rely on her own instincts in ticklish situations and get along better, so in spite of everything the situation turned out for the best. Such are the twists and turns in the healing process.

*   *   *   *

The transforming symbol of the Self is the great mystery that lies hidden in all healing. It appears as a manifestation of God in the soul, and in the body as well. To call this the Self, and describe it as a transforming symbol, is merely to name something that is basically a mystery to us. That which heals us is essentially unknown, though how healing functions can to a certain extent be described. There is an inclination on the part of those engaged in the healing arts to forget their ignorance of these things and, inflated by their grasp of some tiny portion of the mystery of healing, to proclaim themselves prophets. The messianic pretensions of psychological systems in our day is matched only by the messianic pretensions of religious systems in bygone eras. Everyone who finds himself preaching to others the virtues of his latest remarkable discoveries about healing, fanatical in his desire to convert others, needs to know that underneath this are his own unconscious doubts. The healing process can be extremely numinous and so the danger of inflation is always there for patient and healer alike. Only when the therapist remains in touch with his own suffering and needs, and therefore with his own humanness and limitations, can he avoid the dangers of inflation, and can others be spared having a messianic attitude foisted upon them.

The contribution of Jungian psychology to our knowledge of illness and health is simply that—a contribution. We are only beginning to understand the deepest mysteries of the human psyche and body. Perhaps the greatest contribution of C. G. Jung to this enterprise is not his description of the different components of the psyche—valuable though this is—but his understanding of the methodology along which healing proceeds. I have tried in this chapter to give some of the essence and spirit of the process of healing as it takes place via the interaction of the ego and the unconscious, but ultimately this process defies description. We can talk of the conflict of opposites, the value of becoming conscious, the mediating nature of the transforming symbol, but like many life experiences, healing can perhaps only be truly understood by people who have been ill and then have become well. True, this healing process points to the existence within us of the larger personality of the Self, but even this figure within us will only be approximately understood by us in our earthly lifetime. Jung puts it aptly in the following words, which summarize what I have been trying to present in this chapter, and leave us, as we should be left, standing at the edge of a mystery:

"Psychology therefore culminates of necessity in a developmental process which is peculiar to the psyche and consists in integrating the unconscious contents into consciousness. This means that the psychic human being becomes a whole, and becoming whole has remarkable effects on ego consciousness which are extremely difficult to describe. I doubt my ability to give a proper account of the change that comes over the subject under the influence of the individuation process; it is a relatively rare occurrence which is experienced only by those who have gone through the wearisome but, if the unconscious is to be integrated, indispensable business of coming to terms with the unconscious components of the personality. Once these unconscious components are made conscious, it results not only in their assimilation to the already existing ego personality, but in a transformation of the latter. . . . The ego cannot help discovering that the afflux of unconscious contents has vitalized the personality, enriched it and created a figure that somehow dwarfs the ego in scope and intensity . . . [so that the ego] gradually subordinates itself to the stronger factor, namely to the new totality figure I call the *self*."[11]

Notes

1. As L. L. White has shown in his book *The Unconscious Before Freud* (New York: Basic Books, Inc., 1960), the idea of the unconscious existed in minds of poets and philosophers long before Freud's time, but to Freud and Jung goes the distinction of demonstrating the reality of the unconscious empirically, and using the hypothesis of the unconscious to develop a method of healing.

2. See, e.g., Joseph Campbell, *The Hero With a Thousand Faces* (Princeton, N.J.: Princeton University Press, 1949).

3. From Alan McGlashan, *The Savage and Beautiful Country* (Boston, Mass.: Houghton-Mifflin, 1967).

4. C.G. Jung, *Aion*, C.W. #9,2, pp. 24-25.

5. Cf. the writings of John Perry, M.D., "The Self in Psychotic Process," "The Far Side of Madness," and "Lord of the Four Quarters."

6. C.G. Jung, *Civilization in Transition*, C.W. 10; p. 170. I am indebted to Brewster Beach of New York for calling my attention to this quotation in his fine lecture, "The Loss of the Soul and its Discovery in the Unconscious."

7. *Ibid.*, C.W. 10, p. 170.

8. *Ibid.*, p. 171.

9. For a more complete study of this fascinating novel, see Barbara Hannah, *Striving For Wholeness* (C. G. Jung Foundation for Analytical Psychology, 1971).

10. C.G. Jung, *The Practice of Psychotherapy*, C.W. 16, pp. 181-182.

11. *Spirit and Nature*, Eranos Yearbook No. 1, 1946, pp. 433 and 434.

VI

Healing Ourselves

We have already noted that each of us has a certain responsibility for his or her own physical health. The expert services of the doctor are, of course, often essential, but many doctors would be the first to agree that the health of each person is directly related to his own attitudes, psychological and spiritual state, and health habits. We are beginning to understand that our health may depend upon whether or not we smoke, how we exercise, and the care we take in our diet, and that it is up to us to maintain a healthy physical life.

It is the same with the health of the psyche. The trained professional in the healing arts may be very important at times, but ultimately whether or not a person is psychologically healthy, is becoming whole or not, depends upon that individual's effort, understanding, and spiritual development. Indeed, the doctor of the soul, even more than the medical doctor, knows his limitations regarding his power to "make" someone well, and understands that without diligent efforts from the individual no movement toward wholeness can take place. The healing of the soul requires the individual's active participation. There is no drug and no magic that can make us whole or be a substitute for our own psychologically healthy way of life. It seems, for this reason, only appropriate in a book on healing to point out a *few* of the ways in which people can help themselves in their search for wholeness. I want to emphasize that this chapter will mention only a few of the many paths to healing that are open to us. I am limited here by my own experience and capacities, and also by the patience of the reader.

Relationships

The development of consciousness is not possible without emotion, and emotion comes to us through the significant relationships in our lives. If we have not loved and hated, been enriched and injured by others, life has not been lived. For this reason relationships are crucial to our psychological development.

These relationships must be of the sort that make us vulnerable to being hurt and open to the influence of others upon us. One danger of both psychology and religion is that one may use them to cheat on life. Life is not lived if everything is psychologized, or everything is pulled into a religious scheme or system. Psychology is of value only insofar as it enables us to live our lives more fully and completely; it is not a goal in itself.

A person who lived on a desert island could not be whole, not only because individual psychological development cannot take place without interaction with others, but also because being a whole person means being a person who is in relationship. Relating to others is part of the process of becoming whole. The whole personality extends beyond the boundaries of a person's individual psychological space and includes others. In fact, our wholeness ultimately may include a relationship to the whole cosmos.

This means, of course, that life must be lived with risk, as the story in Luke 7:36-50, which was discussed in chapter one, shows us. The safe life is not the whole life, and the whole life will have its share of mistakes. Not only will we learn through these mistakes and errors, but they themselves become a part of our mysterious totality. We are our mistakes, as well as our successes. A life without mistakes is impoverished, although, of course, our mistakes and errors must be redeemed by our becoming conscious through them.

Love is the crucible in which individuation takes place. In our culture, however, "love" is a difficult word, for it has many meanings to many people. To be "in love," for instance, is different from loving someone. To be in love means that part of oneself has been projected onto the other person. A man may see in a woman the reflection of his own projected soul-image (the anima) and he feels "in love" with her. In fact he is only in love with himself until he learns to see and care for the human reality of the particular woman. A woman, conversely, may see her inner spirit, her masculine counterpart in the unconscious (the animus) projected onto an outer man who becomes the screen on which her masculine image is reflected back to her. She will then feel fascinated and drawn to that man and experience an "in loveness" with all of its magical quality. To love someone, on the other hand, is to be in possession of one's own self, and to perceive the other person as he or she actually is and to care for this person as a human being who means a great deal to us. In the former case there is an unconscious identification with the other person; in the latter case there is a discriminated relationship. Often the experience of falling in love plays a valuable role in drawing us into relationship, but inevitably, as the human qualities of the relationship ᵢmerge, the experience of being in love recedes. Then it becomes necessary for the relationship to develop on different lines. Whether or not that happens will depend on whether there is an actual human basis for the relationship in the first place, and on the maturity of the people involved.

To love someone is to be affected by that person on an emotional level. We can be healed, helped, wounded, enriched by people whom we love. When we are angry at someone we love we are affected by that too; we will experience the cross of our own opposites in our relationships because love and hate, joy and anger, will be mixed together. Inevitably, having people in our lives whom we love will bring us a measure of suffering and personal conflict, but out of this turmoil of the soul consciousness and wholeness can develop.

Love "softens" the ego and allows in the forces of change. To be incapable of loving means a rigidity or atrophy of consciousness, and in either case the conscious personality diminishes as a result. Through love, anger, and hatred, the powerful, elemental emotions of life, we can be dissolved, injured, renewed, and healed, and the process of personality development can take place.

With all of its admitted difficulties, family life is for many the cauldron of individuation. Children have the capacity to touch upon and expose the most overlooked weaknesses in the parents. Instinctively they touch upon these aspects of the parents' personality that have not been integrated. If the parents, for instance, have not learned how to deal with anger, we can be sure the children will be unconsciously driven to anger them until they learn to accept their own capacity for rage. Children will also compensate for the one-sidedness of the parents. It is no accident that children often wind up with opposing or compensating philosophical viewpoints or attitudes about life. If the parent can avoid being consumed in disappointment or bitterness because his child has "betrayed" him by siding with his adversaries, he can learn much from his child's refusal to identify with his particular form of one-sidedness. Children also expose the parents' shadow personalities. Our overlooked shadows, our incompleteness, our blindness may show up in the children, may even be a contributing factor to the suffering our children may have to endure. In our children we see our mistakes, our unconsciousness, our weaknesses reflected back to us, often painfully, but always as a golden opportunity to see ourselves as we truly are.

A lasting relationship between a man and woman is also a means for individuation. For a man and woman to work through the difficulties that develop between them and establish a lasting relationship, they have to become conscious of many factors within themselves and undergo a process of maturation. For instance, the previously discussed projected images of the anima and animus can best become conscious through a lasting relationship with a member of the opposite sex. The difficulties, misunderstandings, entanglements, joys, and sorrows of a relationship with the opposite sex become the fire in which the whole personality can be forged, so long as we do not flee from such relationships the moment the going becomes difficult. Usually such a relationship occurs in marriage, but this is not necessarily the case, for people who are single may also have significant lifetime relationships with members of the same, or opposite, sex.

An analysis of the relationship between men and women, parents and children, and friends, goes beyond the scope of this book, but it has been necessary to include this brief synopsis of these relationships and their importance because without some significant relationships in life, the stuff of consciousness and the energy for individuation will not be present. The aids in becoming conscious that will be discussed in the rest of this chapter must be viewed in this light. They are aids if life is being fully lived, but not substitutes for the living of life itself, with its demands, complexities, hurts, and joys.

Keeping a Journal

The ancient alchemists tried to transform an original substance, which they called the "prima materia," into the perfected substance, the coveted *lapis* or "philosopher's stone," which not only had the power to change base metals into gold, but also bestowed upon the alchemist himself all manner of spiritual blessings. C. G. Jung has shown that the alchemical "opus," that is, the work of transforming the *prima materia* into the perfected substance, embodied, in projected form, the symbols of individuation. The highly prized *lapis* symbolizes the whole man, and the *prima materia* is the original stuff of human nature that is found in the unconscious of each person.

In order for this process of transformation to succeed, all the elements must be placed within the alchemical retort or *vas*, and then heat must be applied. It was essential that, during the succeeding transformations the initial substance went through en route to becoming the stone, nothing be allowed to escape from the retort. If any of the transforming substances escaped, all was lost and the stone would not be formed. For this reason the alchemical *vas* was tightly sealed.

Psychologically, this tells us that if we are to become whole our psyche must be contained. This means that the different aspects of the unconscious must be recognized and, as it were, "held" by consciousness and not allowed to slip away. When people are unaware of their own nature there is no container for their psyche. Psychic material escapes their attention since they take no responsibility for their moods, fantasies, and opinions, and aspects of their personality are not recognized as their own but are projected onto others.

One way to provide a container for the psyche is to take note of our dreams and not allow them to vanish upon awakening. We can also pay attention to our fantasies, and learn to observe all the strange thoughts and images that cross our minds; in short, to recognize the images, thoughts, and intuitions that continually find their way into consciousness from the unconscious and, by observing them carefully, to keep them in front of us. Developing a container for our psyche also means that we must withdraw our projections; that is, recognize when we are seeing in someone else an aspect of our personality that has been projected upon that person from our own unconscious. If a man sees a woman as a goddess, or as a witch; that is, if he finds himself fascinated and attracted, or repulsed and repelled by a woman, he needs to know if his reaction is colored by an image of the feminine which has projected itself from his unconscious onto her. The same would be true of a woman who finds herself fascinated, or strangely repelled, by a man. In this way psychic contents are made conscious that otherwise would be lost to us.

In this process, our outbursts of affect, changes of mood, moments of inspiration, wild sexual fantasies, and a myriad of other psychic events are not allowed to seize us, or pass through our minds like a wandering breeze at night, without being noted and watched. This requires cultivating an attitude that helps us observe ourselves even as we are in the midst of our experience. The ego has this capacity to detach itself from its own experiences, as it were, and observe what is going on. When this perspective on ourselves is cultivated it gives us an objective vantage point that permits the total psyche to be contained. It also develops the valuable qualities of psychological reflection and self-honesty. In this way the many different parts of ourselves are seen and, as the alchemists would say, nothing is lost.

A great aid in this process is to keep a Journal. A Journal is not to be confused with a diary. A diary contains details of daily life such as when we got up, where we had lunch, etc. A Journal contains a record of the many things that go through our screen of consciousness, or cross our path on any particular day. Keeping a Journal of this sort aids in developing that objective, observing standpoint that is so essential to becoming whole, and also serves to represent the psychic container the alchemists saw to be so essential if the coveted lapis were to develop.

Many things can go into our Journals. This is the place to record our dreams. Here too we can write down our fantasies, the wild urges and impulses that may have crossed our minds. This is the place to make a brief summary of each day's major psychological episodes, to review in our minds the angry scene we had with someone, or to note down the beautiful experience we had when we met so-and-so. Creative ideas also need to be recorded. If we do this with the sparks of creative thoughts that flash through our minds, they become like seeds we have planted in the ground; being written down enables them to grow and develop. This is also the place to write down those terrible thoughts we have that horrify us: the thought, perhaps, that flashed through our mind that we wished so-and-so would die. Writing such thoughts down serves to depotentiate them and take away their frightening character. It also helps us recognize our shadow, the dark strata of our personality from which such unwelcome intrusions emerge.

A few remarks on fantasy may help us see more of the value of keeping a Journal. Many people believe they have no fantasies, but the truth is that a fantasy is going on within us virtually all the time. We need to differentiate between directed and undirected thinking. Directed thinking is the thought process that we more or less directly control. It is willed thinking, the kind of concentrated thought process we direct, for instance, when solving a problem. Our capacity for this kind of thinking is limited. It is also a relatively new phenomenon in man's history, for primitive people possess little of this ability. Even with the best of us, after a certain amount of time is spent in such directed thinking we must "shift gears" and put our minds into neutral. In sleep, of course, such directed thinking is entirely suspended and, as we know from dreams, the ego becomes just one other element of the total psyche, even as the sun at night is just another star in the sky.

The greater part of what emerges into consciousness comes from the unconscious. We do very little "thinking"; rather, our thoughts are handed to us. The ideas, impulses, affects, emotions, imaginary events, and conversations that we call fantasies stream through us out of their source in the unconscious. This is undirected thinking. It may be especially conspicuous to us, for instance, if we pay attention to what crosses our minds as we take a shower, or what we find ourselves dwelling upon when we are driving alone on the freeway. Most people pay no attention to the source of the stream of consciousness and so they miss the presence of the unconscious in their lives. To keep a Journal is to begin to reverse this state of negligence and take into account the unseen source of our psychic life.

Keeping a Journal also helps to develop ego strength. The ego is easily swept away by the affects and images of the unconscious. It can become quite helpless in the grip of the unseen forces that emanate from within. Its strength and inner cohesiveness can also be eroded by the harassing outer influences that impinge upon us. The irritations, personal annoyances, and interpersonal conflicts, which make up the lives of most people, have a fragmenting effect upon us. Writing things down in a Journal is the simplest, most basic way of curing ourselves of the psychological infections we pick up in everyday life. Taking pen or pencil in hand and noting down what transpires strengthens the ego's hand both in dealing with our outer life and with the demands of the unconscious. It takes great ego strength to become a whole person, for the Self can only rally around a strong ego, and taking pen in hand is one way to develop this strength. It also has the value of being inexpensive. A dollar or two will provide us with enough paper and pencils for many months of psychological work.

Keeping a Journal is sometimes also the simplest cure for insomnia. There are generally two forms of insomnia. In one case we cannot get to sleep at night; our mind is restless, we cannot shut it off, the motor keeps running, so to speak. In the second form we fall asleep, but a few hours later we are awake; our mind is filled with thoughts, anxieties, the unintegrated minutiae of the day before, or the list of things to be done in the day to come. Those who have trouble falling asleep may be helped if they spend twenty or thirty minutes writing in their Journal before going to bed at night. This may also serve to prevent our being awakened in the early morning hours, but if we are, it often solves the problem to get up, go to the place in the house where we do our inner work, and begin to write down everything that comes into our minds. After noting everything that seems to be popping into consciousness we may find we are allowed to return to sleep naturally.

A Journal also helps us to be psychologically honest. One of the greatest obstacles to becoming whole is a lack of psychological honesty. There is a lot about ourselves that we prefer not to see. We prefer to rationalize, blame others for our unhappiness, or some outer circumstance for our chronic state of irritation, rather than look within. Nor do we like acknowledging responsibility for the dark corners of our mind with their uninvited fantasies and urges. The habit of carefully noting down everything that goes through our screen of consciousness helps us overcome the psychological dishonesty that is a part of each of us.

A Journal may also be an aid in creativity. As mentioned before, if we have a creative thought and write it down it is like planting a seed in the ground. Later we will find the creative thought or inspiration has grown and developed; the original idea is now enlarged and comes back to us in an expanded form. This too can be written down and then it in turn continues to develop and grow. We may even prefer to have a special section of our Journal for these creative ideas and the developing awareness that emerges from them. In this way our creativity is increased significantly, for creativity comes from the unconscious and not from the ego. Our word "genius" gives us a clue here. It comes from the Latin *genii* which refers to the tutelary spirit of a person who lives and dies with him and becomes his personal god or guiding spirit throughout life. A person who has cultivated a lifelong relationship with his *genii* develops a creative, expanded personality. The *genii* personifies the creative aspect of the unconscious, and using a Journal to note down sudden inspired thoughts or insights helps us develop the kind of relationship with our inner spirit that leads to creativity in life.

The use of a Journal for developing creativity in writing is particularly helpful. Ideas have a way of occurring unexpectedly and spontaneously. Suddenly we are handed an idea or thought from somewhere. By writing this down, and returning to it later, a process is started between the ego and the creative unconscious. The best writing is accomplished when the unconscious has had a chance to work things through so that the material we are going to write is already written in the unconscious and all we have to do is put the words down on paper and go through the technical work of giving them the correct form. This can be called creating via a process of *incubation*, or applying gentle heat to the creative energies of the unconscious by giving them the correct amount of conscious attention. Keeping a Journal trains us to enlist the aid of the unconscious in our creative efforts, and we soon discover that this is where the true creativity lies.

What applies to writing and lecturing applies to other areas of life as well. Problems in business, engineering, or personal relationships can also be approached in this way. Write down the problem first, note your emotional relationship to the situation, and record whatever possible answers or avenues of approach may occur to you. Come back to this a day or two later and the possibilities of a solution are almost certain to have developed. The wisdom of solving problems in this way is reflected in the old adage "sleep on it." It is a way of saying that problem-solving and creativity flourish best when first we give conscious attention to the situation, aided by writing in our Journal, and then we allow the unconscious time to develop a solution or line of approach.

Nothing seems too small or too great for the creative energies of the unconscious. The history of ideas, for instance, shows that the ideas which have been keystones in human development have emerged in many people at more or less the same time, and that they have a history behind them. For instance, we usually associate the idea of evolution with Charles Darwin, but history shows that many people before him anticipated his ideas in one form or another, and that others of his same era reached much the same conclusion at about the same time. It is as though the collective unconscious is working on a problem and tries to bring into human consciousness some new insight or perspective that will be of great value to all mankind. The gifted person is the individual whose consciousness receives this thought and who is able to put it into the correct form at the right time of history so that the idea reaches into the general consciousness of mankind.

On the other hand, the creative aspect of the unconscious goes to work on seemingly minor problems as well. A friend of mine once bought a fine but slightly used sofa only to discover it was too big to go through the doors of her house. She was greatly discouraged when she went to bed that night with the sofa still outside the house, nonreturnable because it was used. That night she had a dream in which she saw the sofa with the back taken off. In the morning she looked at the sofa to see if the back did separate from the remainder of the sofa, and sure enough it did, easily and neatly. Half an hour later her husband had the sofa safely inside the house, the back having been removed and then reassembled.

One word of caution: a Journal needs to be kept in a private place, unless there is such a level of trust in the household that you can be sure no one else will look into it. A Journal should be a place where *anything* can be written down. To feel this sense of freedom we have to know that prying eyes will not read what we have written. This is to protect others as well as ourselves. Perhaps, for instance, we have been furious with another member of the household and have written down all the dreadful thoughts we had. These thoughts do not reflect our total feeling about the person, but are only expressive of the animosity we felt under the heat of the moment, that we were trying to come to terms with by writing them down, but others who read what we wrote might not understand this and might be hurt.

Keeping a Journal is a simple thing. It is perhaps the most basic form of self-healing that there is. But no one can do it for us. To discover what help we will get from keeping a Journal we must buy a notebook and experiment. Chances are we will find it is the best investment in ourselves that we could have made.

Healing through the Body

A middle-aged client was complaining of his daily fatigue. His work exhausted him, and every day when he returned home he was fragmented. "The only thing which helps me," he said, "is when I climb up the mountain right near my house." It was a modest mountain, really just a large hill, which he could hike up and back in about an hour. "Then why don't you climb it every day?" I asked. "Every day?" he replied in astonishment. "Why, I thought that would be a cop-out, using something as a crutch." I answered, "Every day you become a little bit ill, and every day you need to cure yourself. If this is the way you cure yourself, then do it." My friend now climbs his mountain five times a week, rain or shine, and each time returns renewed. One could say that he cures himself of his psychic ills by using his body. It is a small example of the healing potential that lies in the proper relationship with our physical self.

It should not surprise us that the body has an effect upon the psyche, just as the psyche has an effect upon the body, for both are part of one organism and make up a remarkable energy system. The body and the psyche both generate energy, and the energy of the one fills and sustains the other. The body is a fantastic organism designed to produce energy. The food we eat is the basic fuel and, acting upon this, the remarkable biochemical system of the human body produces a flow of life that becomes available to us in the form of usable psychic energy. It is an energy-producing process we often take for granted until something goes wrong with the functioning of the body, and then we feel it immediately and painfully.

A man in his thirties complained of fatigue which set in late each morning and crippled him for the rest of the day. He would have a certain amount of energy when he first awoke, but in mid-morning it would suddenly disappear leaving him high and dry. One night he dreamt of a great hydroelectric facility that spilled out energy in a rush, and then ceased its flow. This suggested that his body was not producing energy smoothly and in the correct way, for the body, like a generating plant, produces a flow of energy. A physical examination by his doctor revealed a liver condition. With lowered alcohol intake, altered diet to control hypoglycemia, and proper exercise, his body began to function correctly again, and his energy flowed evenly and was available to him during the whole day.

The body is a fantastic organism, but it must be treated with respect. It is the product of millions of years of evolution, and we must understand and appreciate how this evolution has left its mark upon us. Perhaps two things are of central importance: diet and exercise.

The diet of primitive man consisted of lean meat, fish, and vegetables and fruits that grew wild. Later man added cultivated plant food to his diet, especially grains. Processed sugars were not known until very recently, and only used widely in the last century, and fatty meats were not eaten because the wild game that supplied meat to primitive man was lean. It is reasonable to suppose that if modern man sticks to a diet similar to this his body will thrive upon it, but if he varies his diet from this natural one, his body may suffer. For instance, processed sugars do not occur in nature. Glucose in natural foods is released into the bloodstream gradually as the pancreas and other digestive organs break down the natural foods, but processed sugar bypasses the digestive system and enters the bloodstream so rapidly that a counterbalancing overproduction of insulin may be released as a consequence. The result is that the body's balance may be upset. Energy may shoot up with the sudden sugar intake, then plunge down when the insulin is released.

Where food was plentiful, primitive man was generally healthy. Before the white man came, the American Indian, for instance, had practically no heart disease, cancer, arteriosclerosis, or dental problems. Aside from deaths at childbirth, accidents, and war, he apparently lived a long and remarkably healthy life.[1] But when the white man came with his diseases (smallpox, tuberculosis, etc.) and altered diet, the health of the Red Man deteriorated rapidly. To respect the body means to live in the natural way, which includes a natural diet.

A healthy body can do far more than most people imagine. It is especially designed for exercise. Primitive people were capable of extraordinary feats of endurance. The Apache Indians, for instance, thought nothing of traveling seventy miles a day over the roughest terrain, and the Tarahumara Indians of Mexico are still known to run all day. Such feats of endurance are matched by modern athletes, showing that the human body is still capable of remarkable achievements given the right conditions. One of these conditions is that it be used. Everything that is used gains in strength, and everything not used atrophies. Nor is physical exercise something only for men, for women also have the gift of physical endurance. There were many times, for instance, in the Long March of the Chinese Communists, when women excelled men in feats of long, slow, physical effort. A woman's body is as strong as a man's, only it may perform in a somewhat different way.

A human being is an energy system, and energy flows from the body through the psyche and from the psyche through the body. Sometimes our bodies feel languid and dull. We say, "I'm so tired I can hardly move." Our arms are limp and we lack vitality. Assuming that we are not physically ill, we need to remember that it is not the body that is tired but the psyche. The body is intact, but the energy is not flowing correctly. We are like a pool of stagnant water instead of like a rushing stream generating power. The task in such cases is to get energy flowing again.

Sometimes in order to do this we need to use psychological techniques of the sort to be mentioned in the next section, but at other times we need to use our bodies. This is especially apt to be true at the end of the day when the psyche has become fragmented or exhausted. At this time purely mental or spiritual procedures may be of no avail for that kind of energy has been used up. Then we need to turn to the body as a source of energy renewal, much as my friend used his body to climb the mountain each day, and in so doing renewed himself spiritually and physically.

This requires a physical program. Exercise was an integral part of the life of primitive man who had to move about constantly in search of food and perform the many physical duties necessary to maintain his existence. In our day, when we may ordinarily have no more exercise than getting in and out of the car, exercise has to be planned. But some kinds of exercise have more healing in them than others. What kind of exercise will release energy for us will be an individual matter. Women may differ from men in this respect, and there may also be a variance of physical types. The heavy-set endomorphic type may have different physical needs than the slim ectomorph, and the athletic capacities of the mesomorph may not be something that others can duplicate. So everyone must find his own way of using his body according to his needs and natural inclinations. I can only offer a few suggestions.

A middle-aged man complained of the harassing nature of his work. He lived in a narrow groove: off to work each morning, back home in the evening, dinner, several drinks (always several too many), and then to bed. It was hard to help this man find a little "soul," for at that time his psychological outlook was constricted, but finally the thought occurred to me that he could take a walk each evening after dinner. To my pleasure he accepted the idea and began by walking for ten minutes each evening. (At the time that seemed to him like a long time to devote to such a pursuit.) It was remarkable what exciting things happened to him on these walks. He heard birds sing, breathed clean air, saw the stars emerge at night, and thought thoughts he did not know he had. Soon he began to walk fifteen minutes, and then thirty, and then, after he heard of a friend who had a heart attack and whose doctor prescribed long walks as part of his recovery, he began to stretch his walk to an hour. Sometimes his wife went with him, which helped both him and their relationship, and sometimes he went alone, which helped his relationship with his own body and soul. He was not an athletic man, and for him this was his best way of contacting the energy system of his physical self.

One reason this man was helped by walking is because of its rhythmic quality. In walking the heart pumps the blood down through all the extremities of the body and then up again through the system. Energy literally moves through us as we walk over extended periods of time, and along with this there may come a flow of life from the unconscious. A minister friend of mine who had a mission in the remote regions of New Mexico told me that one of the high points in his life came when his car broke down late in the evening fourteen miles from town. He had no choice but to walk during the evening and early morning hours from his abandoned car to town. As he walked along alone on that country road he found himself in what amounted to a state of ecstasy. He and the stars above him were one, and the whole cosmos seemed to surround him and fill him with a flow of life. It was a walk he would never forget.

Jogging and long-distance running are two other forms of exercise that can have a rhythm. The goal here is to achieve a constant flow of energy and feel the rhythm of one's body, and experience the deep, even breathing that comes from such forms of movement. Under these conditions the entire psyche enters into an unusual state. The long-distance runner frequently reports discernible states of consciousness.[2] At first there may be the feeling of effort, then sometimes a brief period of depression, followed by a strange euphoria, and then an unusual state of inner equilibrium is achieved in which all sorts of thoughts flow spontaneously through consciousness. At the same time that the heart pumps blood through the veins and arteries, and energy moves through the body, psychic energy also moves from the unconscious through consciousness and back again. When the total experience ends with a renewing shower, the effect can be like a minor rebirth.

Jogging, however, is a jolting form of exercise and suits certain physical types better than others. For some people jogging may be difficult, and may not have the desired spiritual benefits. Swimming may be a good alternative. Here we have the remarkable healing effect that water has upon us, and, especially for people whose muscles are large and loose rather than lean and tight as with runners, swimming may be the best way to find a communion between body and spirit.

Bicycling is also a form of exercise with good "soul." It too is rhythmic and tends to awaken the child within us, and to put us in contact with our natural surroundings. Bike riders are very aware of the motion of air, and they experience a sense of communion with the scenery they pass through. The only difficulty is that usually the bike rider must be on the lookout for road hazards and traffic, and this disrupts his flow of psychic energy and defeats his attempts to achieve a meditative state.

Games are also energizing. There is magic to a ball. A ball seems to summon something up from the depths of the psyche. We are languid and apathetic until a ball moves toward us and then something stirs and we respond. To make contact with a ball, as in baseball or tennis, can be an integrative experience because it is a coordination of physical movement, conscious concentration, and unconscious instinct. A smooth tennis stroke, a satisfying swing at a baseball, a perfectly coordinated shot at golf, all have a psychologically energizing effect because for a moment body and soul are one. Physical games are also healing because they are a form of play. In play something is done exclusively for its own sake. Play also requires our total attention and screens out, for the time being, the disintegrating anxieties of daily life. Observe how happy and whole children are when creatively engaged in play. There are no behavior problems then and energy moves in them in a wonderful way. In play, even as adults, our inner child is activated and this in itself releases energy.

For those who lack athletic skills there are many other physical ways to find healing. For instance, gardening can be healing. There is something about digging in the earth and helping things to grow that connects us with the earth in ourselves. Gardening also provides access to our fantasy life, for as we dig and plant and fertilize we enter into a certain state of consciousness that allows contents of the unconscious to reach consciousness in a very natural way. For those of us who do a mental type of work, an activity such as gardening is healing because it puts us in touch with the other man or woman in us. People who work with their minds need to find the physical man in them, that is, the farmer, hunter, craftsman, or fisherman. No one can live out of just one side of his psyche; the other aspects of the Self must be contacted too, and for many people this will be done through a physical type of work that, since it is done for its own sake, is also play.

For certain people yoga may be another method of using the body for the purpose of renewing the spirit. Through yoga, energy is diverted inward and a special state of consciousness is attained in which energizing elements from within can emerge. Yoga helps by providing a "system," or a technique that has been perfected over the centuries and has been proven by experience to release energy and transform consciousness. The ultimate aim for the true practitioner of yoga goes beyond an exercise of yoga as a physical technique and strives for the achievement of Brahman, or enlightenment, which corresponds to a release from a bondage to the opposites. For many Westerners this ultimate aim is too strange to our culture to be a valid goal, or, more exactly, the goal of release from the opposites must be achieved more psychologically. But many Westerners nonetheless find that the simpler practices of yoga, revolving around physical techniques, are accessible to them.

I have one friend, who knew next to nothing of yoga, who dreamt of it. "To honor this dream," I suggested, "you need to go and try yoga for yourself." He was almost sixty at the time but he did try yoga, and it has now become a permanent and healing part of his life which he practices for fifteen or twenty minutes a day. Since yoga is not at all theological, that is, no particular belief system is required to practice it and it is not a form of "worship," it is a spiritual exercise that can be integrated by Christians and Jews as well as by adherents of other religious faiths, as suggested in the book *Christian Yoga* by J. M. Dechanet (Christian Classics, 1972).

There is not, after all, a separation between spirit and body. There may come a time when the spiritual self separates from the physical self, and leaves it behind as a person might leave a house behind when called upon to make a journey. Presumably this is what takes place at death. But at least in this lifetime our body is part of our totality. Not only are we called upon to respect the body and its needs, and understand what makes for physical health, but we can find ways to renew psychological and spiritual energy by physical means.

Meditation

Meditation is the art and technique of giving long and concentrated attention to something of personal or religious importance. In its broadest meaning, meditation includes prayer, certain types of painting, meditative reading, and spiritual exercises such as yoga, as well as the more classical experience of inward contemplation.

There is so much already written on prayer that I only wish to add a few comments from the psychological viewpoint. Prayer is "talking to God"; psychologically, this results in an orienting of the ego to the Self. Prayer is an instinct; that is, there is a tendency in us to pray automatically, without having to think about it. For many people the problem comes when they *do* begin to think about it, for at this point they may become plagued by doubts, as well as by a voice within them that tells them they have to go about it in a certain way. On the intellectual side we may doubt that there is any God Who is listening, or our prayers may be interrupted by thoughts such as "Why bother to pray; God knows everything there is to know anyway." These theological and philosophical puzzles have the effect of paralyzing the natural instinct to appeal to a Higher Power.

The curious fact is that the efficacy of prayer is scarcely affected at all by our personal beliefs about God. It does not matter what we believe, but what we do, and a prayer addressed to our version of the Higher Power we call God has much the same effect regardless of our conscious beliefs or disbeliefs. It is the motion of the soul that counts, and prayer is one way to move the soul toward God which is, psychologically, toward the Self or inner Center. This is suggested by Jesus' attitude toward prayer. He didn't concern himself in the slightest with a person's conscious beliefs. We don't read of his asking anyone, "Do you believe in God?" What he was concerned with was a person's faith, which, as we saw earlier, has to do with the motion of the soul, and not with theologies or philosophies.

Perhaps the best way to pray is to be natural. Here is where religious training defeats many people. We read pious, formal prayers in prayer books, or hear a minister intone some special language that seems to be appropriate when the Deity is addressed, as though God does not respond to ordinary talk but only hears and answers when one shifts into some kind of pious discourse. Ritual needs a special language, of course, but on the personal level this makes many people intimidated when it comes to expressing themselves in prayer. Prayer becomes one more skill they feel they do not have, and self-consciousness kills their natural religious instinct.

An example of perfectly natural prayer is Tevye in the musical *Fiddler On The Roof* who talks with God in a delightfully natural way. Tevye simply says to God what is on his mind. If he is upset, he says so; if he is peeved with God, he tells Him so. Being the natural man he is, the pious intonations of the clergy and the sanctimonious books on the subject have not stifled him.

The values of prayer are hard to assess. On the purely psychological level prayers that are natural and spontaneous and contain our real feelings, agony, and concerns have the effect of building a relationship between the ego and the Self. Since the Self is like a personal representation of God in the soul it is no minor achievement to establish such a living relationship. There is no need then to say that this is "nothing but" psychology. If anyone can forge a link between the ego and the Self via prayer he has accomplished a life task of such importance that it is not invalidated by the fact that he has not worked out all of the theological questions involved. For this reason I always encourage people to pray, and to go about it in whatever way is natural to them.

Meditation is akin to prayer but also somewhat different, for while prayer is talking with God, meditation is more the art and technique of developing an unusual state of consciousness for the purpose of inward contemplation. There are many methods and philosophies of meditation. Christian meditation has largely evolved out of Christian mysticism, and involves the contemplation of images from the great storehouse of Christian tradition and imagery. The cross, or the birth of Christ, for instance, may be the object of a contemplation in which it is hoped that the deeper meanings of the Christian images will speak to the meditator to enrich his mind and heal his spirit. The Reverend Morton T. Kelsey in his book *The Other Side of Silence* (New York: Paulist Press, 1976) has given an excellent resume of the place of meditation in the Christian tradition.

In America today forms of meditation derived from Eastern philosophy and tradition are much more popular than classical Christian meditation. Eastern meditation generally seeks to create a void in consciousness as a means of liberating the soul from the world of illusion (Maya) and freeing the personality from the chains of karma so it can become enlightened. Aids in developing this void, such as a mantra, may be used in certain cases. However, since there are already many books on the subject of meditation and Eastern meditation in particular, I wish to confine my remarks to what can be called "psychological meditation," about which there is very little written today.

As with other forms of meditation, psychological meditation

requires the capacity to enter into a different, contemplative state of consciousness. It differs from Eastern meditation because the mind contemplates a definite image, and does not seek the void, and from Christian meditation because the image that is the object of contemplation does not come from a religious tradition but from one's own unconscious. In what follows I will make some suggestions on how to develop the technique of psychological meditation. They are suggestions only, for each person must work out his own way and style, as it is the nature of psychological meditation to be highly individual in nature.

Meditation works when we have achieved a certain state of consciousness; it requires a different level of awareness from that which we need for the ordinary business of living. There is, however, nothing mysterious about it, and most people can achieve this required level of awareness by following certain simple procedures. The first step is to become physically relaxed, and this means finding the correct physical posture. Usually reclining in a chair offers a good possibility for the necessary relaxation. Sometimes we can help our body to relax by talking to it, instructing each part of the body in turn to let go, imagining the tensions disappearing. Yet at the same time we must not allow ourselves to fall asleep, for meditation requires a combination of being relaxed and yet alert. If we do fall asleep, we must plan our times of meditation for the morning, or some appropriate time of day when we are sufficiently refreshed. Each person has to find his own best time for meditation, keeping in mind that it requires considerable energy and we may want to devote our best time of the day to it.

The place where we meditate may also be important. Meditation can, of course, be accomplished in many different places and settings, but quite often it helps to have a particular place which is "our spot" for this sort of thing. This may be a place in the garden, or a particular part of the house which we come to associate with the meditative state. This spot will need to be a place where we are reasonably sure we will not be interrupted.

Many people are blocked from meditation by thoughts that intrude concerning the many things they have to do that day. It is as if we have an inner secretary with a list who keeps reminding us of all these things. If our minds are so cluttered with these details of life that we cannot free ourselves from thinking about them, it may help to write down a list of all the things we must do as soon as we are through with our meditation. Usually this satisfies the inner secretary who lets us alone for a while.

Once we have achieved a relaxed but alert state, and know we will not be interrupted, we are ready to develop the different level of consciousness meditation requires. Actually, we are already on the way to this, for having screened out outer stimuli, laid aside the thoughts of daily life, and become relaxed, we are automatically in a different level of awareness. To go further into that level of awareness we may want to imagine ourselves "sinking down" deeper into ourselves, or perhaps descending a flight of stairs, or, if it seems better to us, ascending a mountain. What we are going to do in our psychological meditation is to contemplate the images that come from our own soul, and what we wish to achieve is a level of awareness in which the light of consciousness is, so to speak, dimmed so that these inner images are more visible. Think of the way a rheostat works. By turning the dial on a rheostat we can dim the intensity of an electric light without extinguishing it. Consciousness also has a certain intensity or light that can be dimmed without being extinguished. The light of consciousness must be dimmed in this fashion or we cannot see the images of the unconscious, just as in the daytime when the sun is bright in the sky the lights of the stars are not visible. The goal is to achieve a kind of twilight state of awareness in which we are awake and alert, but in which the images from within can be seen.

In psychological meditation, as mentioned, the image for contemplation comes from one's own unconscious. An image of this sort might, for instance, be provided by a dream, for dreams offer us many images that invite meditation and contemplation. Or perhaps we will wish to leave our minds free and see what image appears. In the meditative state of consciousness images from the unconscious cross over into our screen of awareness and these are proper objects for meditation or contemplation. Or perhaps we will simply let our thoughts roam through a whole world of inner images that come spontaneously from our storehouse of dreams, fantasies, and memories. Only practice and experience can tell us what will work best for us and how it works. Just as every alchemist had to do his own work for himself, and his Master could take him only so far, so everyone who meditates must perform his own labor and find by experience what is his particular way of working.

In addition to its relaxing effect, meditation has a healing power because of this opportunity for the contents of the unconscious to cross over into consciousness, thereby promoting the function of integration. This enables us to come to terms with troublesome psychic states, and also to develop new sources of energy. Every psychic state, mood, or emotion has an image that goes with it. We may be helpless in a depression, dark mood, or a violent affect, but if we can find an image that corresponds to our psychic state, we can become free of it, for the image has a power to heal.

A woman once called me to complain that she was in a terrible depression. Everything was going well enough in her outer life, but she felt dull, stupid, and dumb. We talked and talked but there seemed to be no answer to her predicament until it suddenly occurred to her to say, "I feel like Lenny in the movie *Of Mice and Men*." Lenny was a dumb brute of a man, an imbecilic character "That's it," I suggested. "It's like your dumb, stupid Lenny of an inner man has gripped you." She took this image and worked with it and came out of her depression. Before she had the image she was powerless, gripped by the dark feeling, but when she had the image that represented her state of mind, she became free.

Meditation releases psychological energy because the images of the unconscious contain energy. Contemplating the images of our dreams has the effect of transferring energy from the unconscious into consciousness. In this way a sterile, empty state of consciousness can become filled—enlivened by the energic contents of the unconscious. But we must do our part by giving energy back to the unconscious via our concentration. It is part of the law of reciprocity in nature. If we take out we must put in. If a farmer takes out the life of the soil in raising his crops, he must also give life back to the soil by fertilizing it. So we must expect to give energy to our inner life at the same time we receive energy from it.

There is also the possibility of doing what can be called "guided meditation." If we lack energy, for instance, we can imagine energy flowing into us. Perhaps we "see" energy streaming into us through the soles of our feet, working its way up through our bodies like an electric current, passing outside of us through the head and then completing a circle and returning through the feet. It is best to represent this flow of energy as a circle of energy in constant movement because energy *is* movement. We cannot "store it up" for long, but must continually express energy and receive new energy.

It is also possible to use guided meditation for the purposes of healing the body. We can imagine our bodily condition, then see the natural healing forces of the body going to work and routing out the enemy of illness or malfunction, and, finally, see ourselves restored to a whole state, running or walking with vigor and health. Carl Simonton, M.D., of Fort Worth, Texas, is doing research now on the possibilities of such a type of meditation for healing cancer. Three times a day Dr. Simonton has his patients visualize their disease, then "see" in their minds the antibodies within them repelling the cancerous cells, and then imagine themselves whole and healed.

Meditation can also be done in connection with certain kinds of reading that are related to our inner situation or development. In order to do this kind of meditative reading we will study a page or two of written material until something strikes us that is provocative, and then let our thoughts drift around what we have read. In this way certain insights are likely to emerge into consciousness as the unconscious makes connections between what we have read and our present psychological situation.

Of course this only works when we are studying the right book. I am always impressed, however, by the way the right books find their way to us when we are engaged in the process of becoming whole. Maybe we are in a bookstore and a certain book jumps out, as it were, to meet our eye. Or perhaps a friend suggests a book that proves to be just what we need at the time. Or it may be that our dreams will suggest a certain line of reading. We can always tell when we are doing the right kind of reading because the material will interest us. If we have to read and reread something, still hardly knowing what we have read, either we are not ready for it, or it is not related to our immediate process of development.

Many people find their inner-directed reading enriching precisely because it relates to their individuation. Unfortunately, this often conflicts with an educational program in which our reading material is dictated to us by teachers or professors. For this reason more than one person has been compelled to abandon academic pursuits in order to follow an educational program directed from within. It is then a matter of being taught by the unconscious. Individuation, which is growth and development, is also learning and coming-to-know, and the unconscious is the greatest teacher of them all.

Another way of dealing with inner images, which is akin to meditation, is through painting or sculpture. These art forms give visual representation to a psychic image. Some people, for instance, paint certain scenes or images from their dreams. In this way they "live" with the image, and sometimes in the painting certain details emerge that otherwise would have escaped their attention. Such a psychological painting may also release us from a depressed or wretched state of mind.

A young woman with whom I had worked without success for many months was subject to violent times of depression in which she became suicidal. Neither I, nor the many others who had tried to help her, were able to help her understand or work out her depressions, and the situation was very serious and distressing. One night she phoned at 2:00 A.M. with a terrible suicidal urge, and it was all I could do to bring her out of it for the moment and safely through to the morning. When she came to see me the next day we discussed her dark episode of the night before, but were getting nowhere until, when I asked her to describe how she felt, I noticed that she began to move her arms about as she talked. It popped into my mind that I had once heard someone say, "When someone waves their arms when discussing a dream it means that it wants to be painted." So I said, "Paint your mood. Make a drawing of how you felt." This idea met with great resistance, which often happens when an unusual sugges-tion such as this is made, but finally she agreed. The next day she brought in a most remarkable drawing. It was about two by three feet, full of darkness and great jagged lines, but also with a strong human figure in the center and light seemingly breaking through the darkness here and there. We never did "understand" her depression, but this painting broke the back of the dark spell that had been cast upon her and she was no longer so gripped by despair that she was in danger of taking her life.

The important thing with such painting is, of course, not the finished product but the process. Many people are blocked from using their creative imagination or skills because they are so oriented to the finished product. Something in them constantly stands in judgment and criticizes what is being written, painted, or sculpted, and the ef-fect of this is to block spontaneity; in fact, it may stop us in our tracks and prevent any effort at all. It is important to identify such a critical, judgmental voice, and know when the critical-person-who-looks-over-our-shoulder is talking down our efforts. Such a voice will say certain typical things such as, "That isn't any good," or "What you are doing is foolishness," or "People will laugh at you." It is es-sential not to follow this voice. We must make it understand that it does not matter whether or not what we are doing is "good" because we are simply working for its own sake.

The problem is especially difficult with trained professionals. When I suggested to one professional artist that she paint some of her dreams, it met with the objection that her perfectionist side would in-terfere and force her to turn it into an artistic endeavor. So I made the suggestion that she do her psychological paintings with her left hand, for no one could criticize a painting made with the left hand, nor expect it to be anything but what it turned out to be. She did not take me up on this suggestion, but it did liberate her to paint in an en-tirely different way. The psychological paintings that she did in this way were much freer than the paintings she did professionally. The latter were done quite carefully and with great attention to detail, but the former, while outlandish and even grotesque, with lines going every which way, had more vitality and psychological impact.

Meditation, then, is working with an image, and psychological meditation uses an image that has come from one's own unconscious. In meditation the image interacts with the conscious personality in such a way that both are changed. The result is a modification of the conscious standpoint in favor of the unconscious, and a gradual assimilation of the unconscious into the ego structure. In this way images and symbols from the unconscious are used by the transforming function of the psyche.

Sometimes when we give energy to an image from the unconscious in meditation it will begin to move, that is, it will change even as we are observing and studying it. If so, we are at the point where meditation becomes that special psychological technique Jung called "active imagination." It is to this that we now turn.

Active Imagination

Psychological analysis alone is not enough to bring about the healing of the soul. Even though we understand all of our personal past history, and see the forces at work in us that have shaped our lives, this by itself will not heal us. The chief value of such analysis is that it gives us conscious orientation and a certain perspective. It also generally increases ego strength, thus freeing us to make certain choices and find new attitudes. All of this is very helpful, but not enough. Something more must be done in order to reconcile the conscious and the unconscious, to alter a destructive inner situation, or bring new life. This calls for some means of establishing and keeping alive the ongoing relationship with the inner world out of which new life comes and through which eventually our conflicts may be resolved.

One special tool for working with the unconscious that was developed by C. G. Jung is "active imagination." Active imagination goes a step beyond meditation. Meditation, as we have seen, involves the contemplation of an image; active imagination is interaction with an image. The technique of active imagination brings into focus an image, voice, or figure of the unconscious and then enters into an interaction with that image or figure. In active imagination the ego is definitely a participant. We are not passively watching, but are positively involved in what is happening. It calls for an activation of the image from the unconscious *and* an alert and participating ego.

One word of caution: active imagination can start a flow of images from the unconscious that, in a few cases, may be difficult to stop. This can be frightening, for the images are then like a flow of water that cannot be turned off and there is the fear of being inundated from within. I have never known anyone actually to be injured in this way, but I have known one or two people who became quite frightened. This is not likely to happen, for most people can turn off active imagination any time they want to, but it is a possibility if someone is too close to the unconscious and has not sufficient ego strength. In this case active imagination should not be undertaken without the guidance of a skilled spiritual director or therapist with whom the experiences can be shared if necessary.

Active imagination can begin in several ways. A dream is one place to start. In this case we continue the dream in our imagination as a story, writing down whatever comes to us. This is especially helpful in certain dreams that do not reach a conclusion. For instance, maybe we dream we are being pursued by some figure; we run and run and the dream suddenly ends while we are still running from this figure. This is an "unfinished" dream. It does not end because the unconscious cannot take the action any further. We can continue the dream by finishing its story in active imagination. What happens now as that figure pursues us? Perhaps we see ourselves stopping and facing our adversary, or maybe someone comes into the situation to help us. Any number of possibilities present themselves, but only one can be selected and this is the one we will follow through to see where it leads us.

A fantasy can also be utilized as the basis for active imagination. The place to begin would be with the fantasy that has been haunting our minds, the uninvited train of thought that keeps coming back to us again and again. Maybe it is a recurring fantasy of a burglar breaking into our house, or perhaps of some kind of doom descending upon us, or perhaps it is a powerful sexual fantasy. One can take the fantasy and deliberately develop it, writing down whatever occurs to us as we continue the fantasy as a story. This has the effect of altering our psychological situation, and of making clearer the underlying meaning of the fantasy. With sexual fantasies this may be the only way to avoid living them out concretely in ways that may be destructive to our relationships.

One source for Jung's ideas on active imagination was alchemy. Alchemy spoke of the adept (alchemist) giving careful attention to all the elements in his retort and observing their transformation with great concentration. Jung transliterates the language of alchemy into its psychological equivalent and sees this as a prototype of active imagination. What alchemy suggests, he says, is that we,

"Take the unconscious in one of its handiest forms, say a spontaneous fantasy, a dream, an irrational mood, an affect, or something of the kind, and operate with it. Give it your special attention, concentrate on it, and observe its alterations objectively. Spare no effort to devote yourself to this task, follow the subsequent transformations of the spontaneous fantasy attentively and carefully. Above all, don't let anything from outside, that does not belong, get into it, for the fantasy-image has 'everything it needs.' In this way one is certain of not interfering by conscious caprice and of giving the unconscious a free hand." (*Mysterium Coniunctionis*, C.W. 14, p. 526)

In the same volume, on page 495, Jung puts it even more explicitly:

"This process can, as I have said, take place spontaneously or be artificially induced. In the latter case you choose a dream, or some other fantasy-image, and concentrate on it by simply catching hold of it and looking at it. You can also use a bad mood as a starting point, and then try to find out what sort of fantasy-image it will produce, or what image expresses this mood. You then fix this image in the mind by concentrating your attention. Usually it will alter, as the mere fact of contemplating it animates it. The alterations must be carefully noted down all the time, for they reflect the psychic processes in the unconscious background, which appear in the form of images consisting of conscious memory material. In this way conscious and unconscious are united, just as a waterfall connects above and below."

Active imagination can be started from any manifestation of the unconscious—dream, affect, mood, or whatever—but the simplest place to start is with the daily running dialogue that goes on within the minds of most of us. We spend a lot of time "arguing" with ourselves. A little introspection will reveal that there are all kinds of voices battling inside of us. Often these inner dialogues resemble courtroom scenes, and it is as if we are on trial for something. There is the inner prosecutor, the critical voice that tries to convict us of this or that, and that also, as a rule, constitutes itself as judge as well as accuser. In a woman this voice usually has a masculine character, and in a man a feminine character. These "voices" are like autonomous thoughts or moods that suddenly inject themselves into our consciousness. If we are totally unaware of them, we become identical with them. If the "voice" we are hearing is the accusing voice of the inner critic or "prosecuting attorney," we become depressed, and our self-image goes down to zero. To become aware of the autonomous nature of these voices is to begin to make a distinction between us and them, and this dawning awareness brings the possibility of breaking free of what amounts to a state of being possessed.

To begin an active imagination with the argument we are hearing inside of us we start by writing down the thoughts already racing through our minds. It helps to personify the different voices we hear. The "Prosecuting Attorney," the "Great Score Keeper," the "Cynical Bystander," the "Forlorn Woman" are personifications of inner voices that certain people have used from time to time. The personification should, of course, correspond to the kind of voice we are hearing. Transferring the inner argument to paper makes it possible for us to respond to these autonomous thoughts, and encourages us to clarify and adopt our own point of view. By writing things down we really begin to hear what is being said, and are now in a position to examine these utterances for what they are. In doing this we may discover that the authority of the inner critic, for instance, may not be so great after all, that while this critic poses as God it is actually a personification of collective opinions, that is, of general or conventional points of view.

Writing things down also strengthens the ego, for to take pen in hand and begin to write is an ego activity, and has the effect of solidifying and centering consciousness, and affirming it in the face of destructive influences. Hence it now becomes possible to find our position and, perhaps, turn the tables on an inner enemy who, up until now, has had the advantage of being able to work in the dark.

Of course it can also be a positive voice we hear and with which we learn to talk. Just as there is a negative voice that seems to want us to fail in life, so there is a positive voice that gives us helpful insights and flashes of inspiration. We can cultivate a relationship with this side of ourselves by learning to dialogue with it, and talk over with it our life situation.

The ancients used to call such a figure a "spiritus familiaris." Socrates referred to it as his "daimon," meaning not "demon" in the negative sense of the word, but his "genius" or inspirational spirit. In

Christian parlance it is a version of the guardian angel or a manifestation of the guidance of the Holy Spirit. Psychologically this positive
figure can be likened to a personification of the Self as it relates to
ego consciousness. If a relationship with this inner figure can be developed, we are greatly helped. It is like having an inner analyst or
spiritual director. In some cases it is the way to freedom from depen-
dence on an analyst, for it gives us access to our own unconscious
wisdom.

Notice how many times I have said that in doing active imagination we must write it down. There are many reasons for the importance of putting active imagination in writing. Writing gives reality to
it; unless it is written it may seem wispy and vaporish and lack impact. Writing things down also keeps us from cheating on the process.
It may be that there are some unpleasant things we have to learn
about ourselves and it is easy to avoid these unless they are written.
Writing also, as mentioned, strengthens the hand of the ego and develops our conscious position in the face of the unconscious. Finally it
gives us a permanent record and enables us from time to time to
review what we have done. Not only does this refresh our memory,
but there are times when something has emerged in active imagination that we could not understand at the time but is clear to us later.

There is one exception to the practice of recording active imagination: sometimes it works best when we are in a meditative state,
and writing it down might interrupt. Pursue the active imagination
while meditating, but then record it immediately in the Journal.

I mentioned the risk in doing active imagination, but the greater
difficulty lies in getting people to do it at all. Some of this has to do
with the fact that it must be written to become real. To write down
active imagination is work. In fact, active imagination itself is hard
work; it takes discipline, and to do it we must overcome the inertia
that grips us when it comes to psychological matters. People are lazy
about their own psyches. We do not want to have to work on ourselves, but want everything to come to us. This is a common difficulty
the therapist encounters: he finds that people come to him expecting
him to have some magic with which to make everything all right, and
they won't have to do the work themselves. Not only is this exhaust-
ing for the therapist, who has to provide more than his share of
energy for the process, but the client does not make satisfactory
progress, for the fact is that we get well in direct proportion to the
energy we put into our psychological development.

In addition to the lazy streak in us, which resists doing active
imagination precisely because it is "active," there is also the voice

within us which is certain to comment that it is "nothing but your own thoughts." As soon as we depart from the known and conventional, this cynical, doubting voice begins to comment that what we are doing is nonsense, banal, or not worth writing down. It is another aspect of the critical voice we have met before, and may also say to us when we awaken with a dream, "Oh, that dream doesn't mean anything." People who try to do creative writing are certain to run into this voice too, and will hear it say things such as, "Oh that has already been written," or, "You will never be able to get it published." This voice will try to keep us from doing active imagination, and will make poisonous comments as though it wants to keep our development on the most mediocre level possible. It acts like a negative mother voice in a man, or a poisonous father voice in a woman, a version of the witch who, in fairy tales, paralyzes the young hero or heroine, turning them into stone, or sending them into sleep, or causing them to lose their heads.

There are two ways to deal with this voice as it relates to active imagination. One method is to resolutely go ahead anyway, to say something like, "I don't care what that voice says, I am going to do this active imagination and when it is done we will see what it is like." The other method is to begin the active imagination by dialoguing with the voice itself. If we have it out with this voice to begin with we may find that the battle is half won and we are beginning to free ourselves from something paralyzing that has affected us on many levels of our life.

In the dialogue form of active imagination it often works best to write down the first thoughts that come into our minds. We identify the voice with whom we wish to speak and say what we want, and then record the first "answering thought" that occurs to us. Then we answer back, and so the dialogue proceeds. It is important not to criticize or examine what is being said as we go along, but to proceed as if it were a normal conversation. Later, when it is all finished, we can go back over what we have written and examine it for some of its content if we wish.

Active imagination sometimes has more vitality than other times. There are times when an image, voice, or fantasy is right there and becomes activated at once and interacts with us. At other times the results may not be so vital. Some people, for instance, may be able to do active imagination in the morning, but not in the evening. For others it may be the other way around. Each person must find his own way of working and discover what suits his personality best.

Active imagination can be very long or very short. A good example of a long active imagination is found in Gerhard Adler's book *The Living Symbol* (New York: Pantheon Books, 1961) in which Dr. Adler discusses a series of active imaginations a woman did over many months, out of which there evolved a long and elaborate fantasy. On the other hand, active imagination may also be quite brief. The shortest active imagination I know of came to a writer who was attempting for the third time to revise a manuscript to please his publisher. Previously he had been able to make certain changes, but this time when he sat at his typewriter absolutely nothing came. For three days he was in depression as not a single thought or word came to him, although usually words flowed like water. At last it became clear that something in him was resisting revising the manuscript, so he decided to personify this resistance and talk to it. The resulting active imagination went like this:

Author (to his resistance): "Okay, why are you resisting doing this work?"
Answering voice (immediately): "Because it is already written."

That was it; there was nothing more that needed to be said. With this the author realized that the book was in its proper and completed form as it now stood, and if the publisher with whom he was corresponding did not want it that way he had to find another publisher. And this is exactly what happened.

Ultimately active imagination is helpful because it tends to reconcile the conscious and the unconscious. It takes us into a relationship with the figures of the unconscious, "negotiating" and working things out with them. This helps bring about that paradoxical union of the conscious and unconscious personalities that corresponds to what the alchemists called the "unio mentalis." Just as the alchemists, in the search for the stone, started with materials that were commonly rejected, so we start with the otherwise rejected material of the unconscious and, through meditation or active imagination, activate an inner process. Jung, in a commentary on alchemical symbolism, gives us this apt description of how this process works to bring us closer to wholeness:

"Thus the modern man cannot even bring about the *unio mentalis* which would enable him to accomplish the second degree of conjunction. The analyst's guidance in helping him to understand the statements of his unconscious in dreams, etc. may provide the necessary insight, but when it comes to the question of real experience the analyst can no longer help him: he himself must put his hand to the work. He is then in the position of an alchemist's apprentice who is inducted into the teachings by the Master and learns all the tricks of the laboratory. But sometime he must set about the opus himself, for, as the alchemists emphasize, nobody else can do it for him. Like this apprentice, the modern man begins with an unseemly prima materia which presents itself in unexpected form—a contemptible fantasy which, like the stone that the builders rejected, is 'flung into the street' and is so 'cheap' that people do not even look at it. He will observe it from day to day and note its alterations until his eyes are opened or, as the alchemists say, until the fish's eyes, or the sparks, shine in the dark solution. . . .

"The light that gradually dawns on him consists in his understanding that his fantasy is a real psychic process which is happening to him personally. Although, to a certain extent, he looks on from outside, impartially, he is also an acting and suffering figure in the drama of the psyche. . . . If you recognize your own involvement you yourself must enter into the process with your personal reactions, just as if you were one of the fantasy figures, or rather, as if the drama being enacted before your eyes were real. It is a psychic fact that this fantasy is happening, and it is as real as you—as a psychic entity—are real. . . . If you place yourself in the drama as you really are, not only does it gain in actuality but you also create, by your criticism of the fantasy, an effective counterbalance to its tendency to get out of hand. For what is now happening is the decisive rapproachement with the unconscious. This is where insight, the *unio mentalis,* begins to become real. What you are now creating is the beginning of individuation, whose immediate goal is the experience and production of the symbol of totality." (*Mysterium Coniunctionis*, C.W. 14, pp. 528-529)

While Jung is the one who first developed active imagination as a psychologically refined tool for working with the unconscious, it has been used before. A very good example of active imagination is found in Matthew's Gospel in the story of the Temptations in the Wilderness (Mt. 4:1-11 KJV). Jesus has gone into the wilderness to be alone after receiving the Holy Spirit from God and hearing the voice that proclaimed "This is my beloved Son, in whom I am well pleased."

Naturally the first thing that would happen after such an experience is an inflation, a temptation to take the experience in the wrong way, and this temptation is presented in the voice of Satan who says "If thou be the Son of God, command that these stones be made bread." Jesus hears that voice within himself and answers it. The voice then speaks a second time, and a third, and each time Jesus hears the voice and replies to it. This is active imagination. Nor is this a way of saying that the Satan in the story is not real. Such a voice within us is *very* real, so real that unless we hear it, recognize it for what it is and respond to it, we will likely be taken over by it. Had this happened to Jesus his whole life would have gone the wrong way. His dialogue with Satan was the cornerstone of the life and ministry which he built and is a vivid illustration of how vital active imagination can be.

Finally, note that the term is *active* imagination. It is not a technique in which the movements of the unconscious are simply observed. Rather the ego asserts itself in the process, and the demands of the unconscious must be measured against the reality of the ego. In his dialogue with Satan, Jesus' ego was very evident. He did not just hear the voice, but reacted to it and responded to it. Of course the dialogue might be with a helpful voice too, such as the dialogue Elijah had with Yahweh's voice in the cave on Mt. Sinai (I Kings 19:9). But in either event the process of active imagination calls for active participation by the ego, and represents an attempt of consciousness and the unconscious to have it out with each other and work out together a creative life.

Dreams

The final matter to be considered in this book is the healing power of dreams. One reason for reserving this topic for the last is because it is so rich and so complex. In fact, it deserves a separate book all its own, so I will only be able to touch briefly upon the subject of dreams in this volume. What I will do is comment on why dreams have healing power and on practical things we can do with our own dreams, and offer some thoughts on how dreams could become a living part of our culture.

"Understand that thou art a second little world and that the sun and moon are within thee, and also the stars." So wrote the early Christian sage Origen as he described the microcosmic world within man.[3] One reason that dreams have healing power is because they give us a picture of this vast and complex inner space that makes up the whole man. We have already noted the healing power of the image, which heals by giving us a visual representation of our psychological state, and thus makes it possible for us to integrate our psychological experience.

Dreams are like stories in which we, the dreamers, are central characters, and basically the stories that unfold in our dreams comprise our stories, the drama of our lives, the saga of our own individuation. By means of these stories, with their vivid images and compelling emotion, we are enabled to come into conscious relationship with the forces that shape our destiny and make up the Self. Small wonder the Jewish Talmud savs that a dream not understood is like a letter not opened, and that the dream has been called the royal road to the unconscious.

The healing power of the dream also stems from its compensatory relationship to consciousness. We have already seen that wholeness comes as the ego more and more perfectly represents the total Self, but the ego is always partial and one-sided. The healing process of individuation takes place through a continuing series of corrections in our conscious attitude, changes or alterations in consciousness that allow mcre of the life of the unconscious to emerge and to expand the personality. The one-sided adaptation of the ego is continually compensated by the unconscious, so that the point of view of the unconscious can be said to be compensatory to that of consciousness. Naturally, to understand and relate to this compensatory point of view is to be healed by it, and it is the dream that makes this possible, for the dream is like the voice of the unconscious and gives us a visual representation of the compensatory attitude we need. It is this compensating quality of dreams that Emily Brontë refers to when she has her heroine, Cathy, in *Wuthering Heights*, say, "I've dreamt in my life dreams that have stayed with me ever after, and changed my ideas; they've gone through and through me, like wine through water, and altered the colour of my mind."

Dreams are also the main conveyers of the "transcendent functior" of the psyche of which we spoke in the previous chapter. Through tneir images and symbols they build a bridɣe between consciousness and the unconscious, thus enabling a relationship to be established, and energy to flow between the two poles of the psyche. They heal by conveying the stored-up wisdom of life to consciousness, and carry within them vital hints of our future development that enable us to move from where we are now to where we must travel inwardly to become complete people. For this reason James Kirsch said of the dream, "The dream is always true and correct. If we could invariably understand it we should be perfect beings."[4]

Dreams also have the function of "building up the soul." Robert Louis Stevenson says of those who follow their dreams:

"Upon these grounds, there are some among us who claimed to have lived longer and more richly than their neighbours; when they lay asleep they claim they were still active; and among the treasures of memory that all men review for their amusement, these count in no second place the harvest of their dreams."[5]

This soul-building quality of dreams is related to their religious function. All over the world ancient man regarded dreams as sent by God for the instruction or purification of the soul, a view also held by the men and women of the Bible—a fact that is generally overlooked by the church today but that did not escape the attention of Abraham Lincoln who wrote:

"It seems strange how much there is in the Bible about dreams. There are, I think, some sixteen chapters in the Old Testament and four or five in the New in which dreams are mentioned; and there are many other passages scattered throughout the book which refer to visions. If we believe the Bible, we must accept the fact that, in the old days, God and his angels came to men in their sleep and made themselves known in dreams."[6]

The religious quality of dreams comes from their numinosity and their origin in the Self. Each dream is tailor-made to fit the individual circumstances and psychology of the dreamer, and carries a message that, as we have seen, has the potentiality of healing and instructing him. To follow a series of dreams is to be confronted with a much greater intelligence within us than that of the ego, something that devises the wonderfully intricate stories that make up our dreams, plans the cast of characters, and fashions a specific medicine for the malady of our souls.

In the Book of Genesis we find one of the many Biblical stories centering around dreams. Joseph is in Pharaoh's dungeon when Pharaoh's cup-bearer and baker are cast into prison with him. Things were never too good in the dungeons of Pharaoh, but one day Joseph observes that the cup-bearer and baker are more depressed than usual. "Why these black looks today?" he asks them. They answer,

"We have had a dream, but there is no one to interpret it." Joseph answers, "Are not interpretations God's business? Come, tell me." (Gen. 40:7-8)

So Joseph regarded himself as an interpreter of dreams, which ultimately proved fortunate for Pharaoh and the whole realm of Egypt. But the story also speaks of the difficulty in interpreting one's own dreams. This is a difficulty that is met with even by those skilled in dream interpretation, for we are in the midst of our own dream and it is hard to get the necessary perspective. It is like being lost in the forest and not being able to see the outline of the forest for the trees, or, as a friend of mine once remarked, "It is hard to see the dragon which has swallowed you."[7] For one who is not trained in dream analysis the situation is, of course, even more perplexing, and we are apt to say therefore that our dreams are "obscure," but the obscurity is in us, not in the dream.

Dreams are like a language. If we wish to learn a foreign language, we know that we will have to expend considerable effort to learn the vocabulary, sentence structure, and way of thinking of the foreign tongue. It would not occur to us to say that the foreign language is obscure, only that we do not understand it. So it is with dreams. If we wish to interpret them we must learn the way dreams are put together, their "grammar" so to speak, and must familiarize ourselves with the kinds of images and symbolic thinking dreams utilize. There is no shortcut to the hard work of learning to understand dreams, and this is no endeavor for the fainthearted or impatient. Nor is there any substitute for apprenticing oneself to a person whose long training and experience have made him knowledgeable in the field.

But fortunately there is much that we can do with our dreams that does not require their interpretation, and we do not have to understand them in order to benefit from them. Note the people whom I have quoted with regard to dreams: Emily Brontë, Robert Louis Stevenson, Abraham Lincoln. These people antedated modern depth psychology by many decades; yet they derived benefit from their dreams. So what I wish to offer are a few practical suggestions on what each person can do with his or her dreams without benefit of professional advice or counsel.

The first thing we can do with our dreams is to write them down. The usefulness of a Journal for this purpose has already been mentioned. Writing a dream down is helpful for several reasons. First it "fixes" the dream in our minds and helps make it a permanent part of our memory. It also gives us a record of our dreams that enables

us to go back over them, see the pattern that is emerging, and the
way the different dreams relate to each other. Writing dreams down
is also a way of giving recognition to the unconscious. It says, "Okay,
I am going to act as though you are real and important to me." The
unconscious respects this. Something in us *knows* when we are paying
attention to it and welcomes the relationship that writing down our
dreams offers. To write dreams down is the same as accepting an
offer of friendship or relationship with the unconscious, and this
leads, in turn, to a further development of our relationship with our
own soul. It also tends to help us see more of the dream and its meaning. Quite often in the process of recording a dream details will come
back to us that might otherwise be lost, and ideas will occur to us
that would not otherwise have surfaced. People who get used to recording their dreams find it as natural as brushing their teeth, and
miss their dreams when they have a few nights in which they do not
remember them. They find, as Stevenson said, that their dreams have
become an important part of their memories, and give them a feeling
for the reality of the soul.

Dream recall varies greatly from one person to another. Certain
types of people seem more likely to remember dreams than others.
Introverted people, for instance, probably recall dreams more than
extraverts. A quiet evening at home seems to encourage dream recall,
while too much outer-oriented activity or evenings in front of the TV
or on the phone discourage it. Some people may remember dreams
almost every night, others may recall only one or two every two
weeks, but almost everyone, with practice and diligence, can learn to
recall some dreams.

It is a good idea to have a pad and pencil by your bed so that
whenever you awaken you can catch hold of your dream image and
jot it down, no matter how unimportant it might seem at the time. If
a voice seems to say to you, "Oh, that is not important, don't bother
with that," pay no attention, but record everything you remember.
Chances are that as you do so other bits of the dream will begin to
come to consciousness until finally you have the whole thing. Some
people find it necessary to write the entire dream down in the night as
it occurs, but it is also possible to make notes on it and reconstruct it
in the morning. Everyone must find his own way.

After the dream has been recorded, the next step is to walk
around in it and, as James Hillman of Zurich has suggested, make a
friend of it. Remember that the dream is like a story or parable and
that you, the dreamer, are involved in it. Explore your own story.
Look around in the dream and go over in your mind what has happened. Ask yourself what it felt like to be in that dream. Did you ex-

perience fear, joy, beauty, curiosity? What were the figures like who appeared to you? Did you like them or shun them? Talk to yourself about your dream experience, and look around in the corners of it, just as you might mull over an experience that happened to you in outer life.

The third step is to associate to the dream. Ask yourself what you think of in connection with the various dream characters, or the objects that you experienced. Write down what first comes into your mind in connection with the different figures or symbols of your dream. Quite often, after you have associated to the different components of the dream, its meaning becomes clearer to you and you will be more related to the dream. Remember that the healing power of dreams comes largely through their power to build a relationship between the conscious personality and the unconscious, using the dream images as a bridge. By associating to the dream images, you help construct this inner bridge that connects you to your own soul. This is work, of course, but nothing worthwhile ever comes without work, and no bridge was ever built without effort being expended.

A fourth step in working with your dreams is to use them as objects of meditation or active imagination. These techniques have already been discussed, so little more needs to be said, except to emphasize that when we use a dream symbol or dream story as the basis for a meditation, we are working with an image that has come from our own soul. This means that the image has an unusually strong connection with the Center of our being. Prayer can also be used in working with dreams. If there is a dream figure who needs help—a retarded child perhaps, or an injured man or forlorn woman—we can pray for this dream figure just as we might pray for an outer person who is in difficulty. The unconscious will respond to the energy and concern we are devoting to it, and our prayer will have the effect of calling into play the positive and creative forces within us.

It also helps to ask ourselves questions, such as why did this dream come to me? Does the dream come to compensate something that is lacking in consciousness? Does it show me an unpleasant side of myself I have avoided? Or does it affirm me by showing me something in a positive light? Does it offer to fill a blank spot in consciousness, or surprise me with something totally unexpected? Does it comment upon some choice or decision I am making, or, possibly, see something about the way I lived the day before that I have overlooked? If we can answer the question of why the dream came, we have made a significant step toward integrating the viewpoint of the unconscious into our consciousness.

Finally, we can discuss our dreams with a friend or spiritual director. Naturally it helps if we have a relationship with an experienced dream analyst, but it is also helpful to talk over our dreams with someone even if that person is not a professional in the field. There was a time when the church provided spiritual directors for matters of the soul, such as dreams; I believe the French called them "directors of conscience," and now and then such a person can still be found, but for most people the one to listen to our dreams will probably be a good friend, or perhaps one's husband or wife.

Of course it must be a particular kind of friend. A friend is a person who will accept us even though he sees all our dark corners. We can afford to let down our masks with our friends knowing that we can trust their acceptance. A friendship goes as deep as this level of trust. With some people we are "friendly," but are not friends. There is a bond between us that creates a climate of cordiality, but it does not go deeper, for we would be reluctant to share our dark secrets. The more we can share with a person the deeper is the friendship. Such a relationship then becomes a "soul" relationship. It is with this kind of person that dreams can be shared.

This assumes, of course, that our friend or companion in dream-sharing will listen to our dreams in the right way. "Do not cast your pearls before swine," Jesus said, and the reason for this is that swine do not know the difference between pearls and ordinary food so they eat everything. We cannot share the pearls of the soul with people who do not respect these things and have a proper feeling for them, for such a person will devour them, not necessarily because that person intends anything malicious but simply through ignorance.

A friend is also someone who will not inflict his shadow on us. If that happens, the friendship is broken. Obvious examples of the way one person can inflict his shadow upon another are: stealing from us, borrowing money and not returning it, making love secretly to our wife or husband, or gossiping about us behind our back. In a friendship the level of trust is deep enough so we know that these things will not happen. This means a certain amount of psychological development has taken place. One has little control over a shadow personality that is not recognized. A friend with whom we share dreams must, therefore, have achieved a certain level of spiritual and psychological consciousness. Otherwise such sensitive material as dreams cannot be "held" in the proper way and the other person's shadow will misuse the information and injure us with it some way.

In discussing dreams with a friend it is usually best to agree that no interpretation of a dream will be made, or, if it is made, will be offered only very tentatively as a suggestion. It is destructive to tell a dream and have someone leap in with an interpretation that may not be accurate and, worse yet, may simply reflect that person's blind spots. The value of telling dreams to a friend is not to have an interpretation, but so we can relate better to the dream. In telling it, we replay it in our minds. The dream story lives again in us and the dream becomes a deeper part of our experience. In the process of telling the dream we may also find that many insights occur to us that otherwise would not have come. We have, so to speak, "turned on the faucet" by telling the dream, and all kinds of things now come welling up from within. The value of the friend is that he listens to us in the right way, and perhaps aids our inner process by asking certain questions concerning how we felt about this or that, not that he "has the answer."

This is especially true if we are in a dream group, that is, where a number of people meet together to discuss dreams. Here it may be important to observe the rule that while people can make suggestions or comments about dreams, interpretations as such are ruled out. Even professional dream analysts learn that in offering interpretations of dreams it is best to offer them as suggestions, and not be apodictic about it, for in the last analysis, as we have seen, only something in the dreamer knows what the dream means.

There was a time when dreams were part of everyday life. The American Indians, for instance, had a "dream culture," in which everyone paid attention to dreams as a matter of course. While there were shamans who specialized in dreams, it was nevertheless also true that dreams belonged to everyone, and were regarded by everyone in the community as helpful manifestations of the spirit world. An excellent study of such a dream culture can be found in Kilton Stewart's fine article "Dream Theory in Malaya."[8] Until the last fifty years or so, dreams in our society were despised and rejected, except by unusually gifted people like Stevenson, Lincoln, Brontë, Dostoyevsky, and others who instinctively knew that dreams were a meaningful part of man's life and experience. Even today most people have little use for dreams and, at best, regard them as something only for analysts and psychiatrists to use in treating "sick" people. The church, sadly enough, has shown little interest in dreams even though dreams were once an important part of Biblical and early Christian experience.

Perhaps the time has now come when this situation can and must change. There seems to be a stirring among people today, a spiritual restlessness, a growing awareness that something is wrong, something is lacking, and with this there is the beginning of a revival of interest in dreams. There is no reason why dreams should be relegated to the consulting room of the doctor. They are as natural as breathing, an integral part of the life of our spirit and soul, and they belong to everyone. Just as individuals are more complete if they relate to their dreams, so a culture will be more whole if it becomes a dream culture. Our culture needs dreams badly. We are a spiritually deprived people. Our souls are hungry, and if we are not filled with the right food we will fill ourselves with the wrong food. Man cannot go empty for long. It is a marvelous thought that every night the Spirit sends us food for our souls in the form of dreams. "Man does not live on bread alone but on every word that comes from the mouth of God," Jesus once declared, (Mt. 4:4) and dreams may be the most frequent and important way in which the Word of God is spoken.

Notes

1. Cf. Virgil J. Vogel, *American Indian Medicine*. Longevity records of people like the American Indians are, of course, lacking, but there are many examples that indicate that the Red Man lived as long as a white man today, in spite of the lack of modern medicine. Vogel writes, "A summary of the opinions of recent studies of aboriginal health and healing indicated that rheumatism and arthritis, dysentery and other digestive disorders, intestinal worms, and eye disorders were present. There were mastoid infections and respiratory ailments, but disorders caused by vitamin and mineral deficiencies were uncommon and were localized. Neurological and psychic disturbances, heart disease, arteriosclerosis, and cancer were rare" (p. 151). The lack of the last three forms of illness may be directly attributable to the physically vigorous way of life of the Indian, and his diet of natural, unprocessed foods. Examples of extreme old age among Indians are frequent. Opechancanough, for instance, who led the Powhatan Confederacy in rebellion against white settlers in Virginia in the early 17th century, led the vigorous Indian resistance for many years until his death at the age of 99. Even then he did not die until he had been captured by the whites, when he succumbed a few days after his imprisonment.

The fact is, where we do have adequate records of Indian life we hear of remarkably long-lived people. There is, for instance, the story of Tay-Bodal, the Kiowa Indian surgeon, who lived to be over 100 years old (cf. Wilbur Sturtevant Nye, *Bad Medicine and Good* [Norman, Okla.: The University of Oklahoma Press, 1962], pp. 105ff), and the Apache Indian shaman Dee-O-Det, described by Ciyé "Nino" Cochise in his book *The First 100 Years of Nino Cochise* (London: Abelard Schuman, 1971), who lived to be 114.

There is also an interesting statement from a Gaspesian (now Micmac) Indian Chief, who in 1678 commented on French vs. Indian civilization: "It is true that we have not always had the use of bread and wine which your France produces; but, in fact, before the arrival of the French in these parts, did not the Gaspesians live much longer than now? And if we have not any longer among us any of those old men of a hundred and thirty to forty years, it is only because we are gradually adopting your manner of living, for experience is making it very plain that those of us live longest who, despising your bread, your wine, and your brandy, are content with their natural food of beaver, of moose, of waterfowl, and fish, in accordance with the custom of our ancestors and of all the Gaspesian nation." (T. C. McLuhan, *Touch the Earth* [New York: Promontory Press, 1971] p. 49.)

2. Cf. Thaddeus Kostrubala, *The Joy of Running* (Philadelphia, Pa.: J. B. Lippincott, 1976).

3. *Hom. in Leviticum*, 126, quoted by Jung in C.W. 16, p. 197.

4. James Kirsch, M.D., "The Religious Aspect of the Unconscious," *The Guild of Pastoral Psychology*, Lecture No. 1, p. 22.

5. Robert Louis Stevenson, "A Chapter on Dreams," *Over The Plains* (New York: Charles Scribners Sons, Biographical Edition, 1910), p. 208.

6. Jim Bishop, *The Day Lincoln Was Shot* (New York: Harper and Row, 1955), p. 54.

7. Thanks to Robert Johnson of San Diego.

8. This article is included in Charles T. Tart, ed. *Altered States of Consciousness* (New York: John Wiley & Sons, Inc., 1969), p. 159.

Index